HEAD OVER HEELS

A YOGI'S GUIDE TO DATING

A cheeky, mind-blowing roadmap to relationships

Rachel Scott

For information about special discounts available for bulk purchases, sales promotions, fund-raising and educational services, contact info@rachelyoga.com.

www.RachelYoga.com

ISBN: 978-0-9959537-0-3

RS Publications

PRAISE

"The 8 limbs of yoga can you give you some much needed support when navigating the 'wild-west' of relationships. Rachel Scott's book, *Head Over Heels* extends one extra "phantom" limb to mobilize your journey through this bizarre, illuminating and at times humiliating world. Don't lie on your yoga mat inert or uninspired! This book flips lies into truths with its creative, whimsical and emotionally accurate practices."

Jill Miller, Creator of Yoga Tune Up®,
author of *The Roll Model-A Step by Step Guide to Erase Pain, Improve Mobility and Live Better in Your Body*

"With rare courage and insight, Rachel reveals the many paths that we can follow to invert our lives from one of seeking acceptance from others to seeking our wholeness from within."

Bernie Clark, author of
The Complete Guide to Yin Yoga and *Your Body Your Yoga*

"Funny, engaging and super practical...*Head Over Heels* goes beyond just dating and shares how we can use yogic concepts to gain a deeper understanding of ourselves through our relationships. GREAT BOOK!"

Chris Chavez, Global Yoga Teacher and Musician

"Authentic, accessible, and inspiring."

Sarah and Alan Finger, Creator of ISHTA yoga and
author of *Chakra Yoga* and *Introduction to Yoga*

Dedication

To the gentlemen, with gratitude.

Note On Meditation and Yoga Practices

At the end of most chapters, you will find brief meditation and yoga practices that support the reading. These meditation and yoga practices can all be found at www.RachelYoga.com.

Table of CONTENTS

NOTE
FROM THE AUTHOR

Imagine for a moment that you are at a yoga studio. Across the room, you see a very enthusiastic but challenged yoga student. Her name is Gertrude. She is wearing socks. She falls out of tree pose, can't touch her toes, and farted once in happy baby.

Now, let's imagine that your eyes survey the room and you see another student. Let's call her Gwendolyn. Gwendolyn is what we might call a "natural yogi." She can put a foot behind her head. She did a press handstand in her first class. She enjoys the taste of wheatgrass.

If you were to come back to a yoga class in five years, which student would you prefer to have as your teacher? The beautiful, flexible, and talented Gwendolyn? Or the dogged and determined Gertrude?

My recommendation? Gertrude.

See, our friend Gertrude has made every mistake. She has "been there and done that." She has navigated every obstacle and fought for each step of her success. And because she has hit every pothole on her yoga road, she is an excellent guide for helping you to navigate the challenges of your personal journey.

Friends, I am your Gertrude of relationships.

If you asked Gwendolyn to detail the secrets of her relationship success, she might say, "Oh, I met the love of my life when I was twenty-four and bam, we've just been blissfully happy ever since!"

While I may admire Gwendolyn's nonchalance and savoir-faire, my personal journey with love has not been so smooth. To name a few of my personal hiccups:

- Enabling an alcoholic's dysfunction
- Having sex to keep the peace
- Withdrawing to icy silence
- Throwing things
- Fighting, when I should have apologized
- Caving, when I should have stood in my truth
- Dumping good guys
- Being dumped by jerks
- Crying to get sympathy
- Lying
- Divorce

For the last twenty years, I have captained a tiny ship called "Finding The One" and sailed it beyond the known territory to the place labeled "Here Be Dragons." And throughout this crazy adventure, I have practiced yoga. And I have realized the principles of yoga that have helped me on the mat can help *all of us* navigate our wild and untamed relationship journeys with more grace, compassion, and wisdom.

We are all human: very alive, very real, and very flawed. And when you start a new relationship, it's time to bring your whole self forward. Your *best* self forward. And for this journey, you need tools and wisdom that will support you to stand in love, and not fear.

You need the tools of yoga.

Back from my dating travels—and with raw humor and a very full heart—I lay at your feet the lessons that I have learned. May they serve you well.

All names have been changed to honor privacy.

Chapter 1
SEEKING

You know that dream?

The dream where you find the love of your life, have magical adventures, master a rewarding career, and then have a couple of kids? Wrap it up with some financial success and healthy living, and then bam, life is complete!

That dream.

I had that dream. But when I was thirty-nine, my long-term relationship ended over the issue of having children. We finally figured out that I wanted them, and he didn't. There I was: suddenly single, no babies, and pushing forty. My career—which perhaps could have been a consolation prize—felt empty and dull. The big dream—my dream—had gone up in smoke.

I sat in stunned defiance of my life.

How had I come to this? Wasn't I a savvy and smart, modern woman? Wasn't I a good planner and at least *moderately* self-aware? Come on; I was a yoga teacher! Weren't we supposed to be, I don't know, *mindful* about this stuff?

And yet, there I was, blindsided by the results of my choices and wondering how this had all happened.

I felt like a failure.

While on the outside I may have looked like a successful yoga teacher (director of education for a prestigious yoga company, living the dream in Vancouver), inside I felt as if I were missing the greatest opportunity in my life: creating a family.

I'd like to say that this watershed moment prompted a profound journey of spiritual insight where I woke up every day, drank kombucha, practiced yoga for two hours, and found inner peace. In reality, I kicked myself, drank wine, ate popcorn, and watched Netflix.

After a couple of months, I realized that having popcorn for dinner for the fourth night in a row was perhaps an indication that something had to change. After all, there could still be time for kids. Maybe. And if I wanted my future to involve a husband and children, then I was going to have to stop watching *Downton Abbey* and do something differently. I certainly wasn't going to meet someone while I was crying over my popcorn. It was time to step out of my comfort zone.

I squared my shoulders, took a deep breath, and signed up for Tinder, Match.com, eHarmony, Plenty of Fish, The Right Stuff, and OkCupid all in the same week.

My God.

I'd never really enjoyed dating, and *online* dating felt even worse. It was full of unfamiliar pseudo communication in the form of "likes," "winks," and "favorites." There were no rules to follow, no guide maps for help. It was the wild west of human interaction.

Questions abounded:

- Was everyone on Tinder really just there to hook up?

- Did a wink mean that he wanted to talk?

- How should I respond to, "Hey, grrrrl"?

- Should I initiate a chat first or did that make me seem desperate?

- How honest should I be? Would "Yoga Teacher Seeks Excellent Baby Daddy to Knock Her Up Really Fast" be too blunt?

And once I did manage to navigate the texts, IMs, and winks, then came the challenge of actually meeting these guys in person.

Here I was, a veteran yogi and experienced teacher trainer, freaking out and trying to uphold my Zen in the midst of Tinder swipes and Starbucks lattes. I watched in horror as all my unfinished emotional business flooded to the surface: my desire to be "nice" rather than honest, my fear of commitment, my wishy-washy boundaries, my objectification of others.

Although I patted myself on the shoulder for my courage in "getting out there," I felt like I had entered the jungle naked without a machete. Or bug spray.

"You think yoga is hard? Try relationships."
—Beverley Murphy, my first yoga teacher

It was terrible. And it was also wonderful.

I began to see each date as a precious opportunity to practice what I preached on the yoga mat. Could I be accountable for my needs? Could I be centered in the middle of the storm? Could I be both honest and kind? Could I question the ridiculous narratives in my head and instead stay present and open to possibility? Yoga philosophy was coming alive— vividly!—in every coffee date encounter, challenging conversation, and intimate moment.

"The success of Yoga does not lie in the ability to perform postures, but in how it positively changes the way we live our life and our relationships."
—TKV Desikachar

I had come to Tinder trying to find "the one," and instead I wound up finding myself.

DATING

Dating is a weird combination of high and low stakes. It's like a game. After all, you've got nothing to lose by going out on a coffee date. If it doesn't work out, it's no big deal. There's likely another date right around the corner. Another roll of the dice.

Low stakes.

And yet ...

There's also the crazy possibility that this person sitting across from you could wind up being your life mate. You could be with them *forever*.

High stakes.

The thrill of this possibility plus a dose of sexual attraction create the perfect storm for losing our cool. The stakes may be low, but they *feel* really high. Our palms sweat. We wonder if our deodorant is working. We worry about our breath. We stumble over our words. And in those messy and stressful moments, we start to see who we really are.

Svadyaya means "self-study." Wisdom begins with the courage to look at who we really are. From this vantage point, every situation—particularly a scary one—becomes an opportunity to see ourselves more clearly. Each encounter on our dating path becomes an opportunity for self-growth and self-love.

We aren't perfect, and the first step on the transcendental train is a willingness to hold up a mirror and take a good, hard look at what we see. We can only perceive so much of ourselves on our own; we need the external world—and other people—to reflect our unseen facets back.

For thousands of years, yoga has provided this mirror.

And now, unexpectedly, so does dating.

Kriya Yoga

Yoga doesn't just take place on a mat or on a mountaintop; it's happening every moment in our daily lives. *Kriya yoga* (yoga in action) has three parts: self-study, the willingness to be uncomfortable, and surrendering to what we can't control. Dating is the perfect place to practice all three.

This book is for seekers. For those who sense that dating can be so much more than a cattle call for connection. This is for you if you want to—with curiosity and courage—make your quest for a relationship a magnificent opportunity for self-love and personal growth.

Atha Yoganusasanam

"Yoga is now." Yoga is happening right now. And now. And now. Each moment is a fresh opportunity for us to show up. Every moment—profane and profound—is an opportunity for mindfulness and transformation. Even that weird second date at Starbucks.

HOW TO USE THIS BOOK

For each of the remaining chapters, you will link practical, real-life relationship issues with key philosophical yoga concepts so that you can immediately start living your yoga in your daily life. I am raw and real with my own personal stories; these candid anecdotes will help illustrate these principles in action. They may also give you a giggle from time to time. At the end of every chapter, I give you tangible dating, yoga, and meditation practices that will help you deal with obstacles and integrate these ideas.

I recommend spending a week with each chapter to deepen your connection with each set of ideas. Take time to put what you've learned into practice in your relationships and your life. Audio guides of the meditation practices and videos of the brief yoga sequences that I suggest can be found at www.rachelyoga.com. Practice with me as you go!

Through integrating your yoga practice into your quest for love, you will expand your self-understanding, learn to speak your truth, cultivate courageous compassion, and soften more into the infinite vulnerability of your heart. And while following this remarkable process will help you find a rewarding relationship with a loving partner, it will also do something far more important: help you to find yourself.

So let's begin.

"The only reason we don't open our hearts and minds to other people is that they trigger confusion in us that we don't feel brave enough or sane enough to deal with. To the degree that we look clearly and compassionately at ourselves, we feel confident and fearless about looking into someone else's eyes."
—Pema Chödrön

Chapter 2
WHOLENESS

"Bella ... When you were gone, when the meteor had fallen over the horizon, everything went black.... And there was no more reason, for anything."
—Stephenie Meyer, *New Moon*

Confession: I've always had a serious romance problem.

I was the little girl who sat in the forest in my flowy white princess costume, refusing to come in because I knew that a unicorn was going to show up at any moment. I'd squeeze my eyes shut and extend my hands out with a carrot offering, waiting for the unicorn to come and gently take it.

In my tween years, I dreamed that Prince Charming was going to sweep me off my feet, though my vision only lasted up to the first kiss. Then I discovered my sister's secret stash of sexy historical romance novels, and I realized that there was a *lot* more to the story. Reading this racy collection not only drastically improved my vocabulary ("rogue," "heaving," "ravished," "defiant," "pulsating," "naïve," "obdurate," "titillating," "member," "penetrating"), but it also gave me some pretty far-fetched ideas about sex, love, and romance.

Hollywood didn't help.

I devoured movies like *The Breakfast Club, Sixteen Candles, Pretty Woman,* and any other rom-com that suggested that true love would drop into my lap and knock me senseless. In these movies, every heroine is a damsel in distress, true love always saves the day, and bad guys (vampires, werewolves, or general scoundrels) are actually the good guys who are just waiting to be reformed by the love of the right woman.

"You complete me."
—Jerry McGuire

I bought into the Hollywood fairy tale hook, line, and sinker. Isn't there something intoxicating and delicious in thinking that Mr. or Ms. Right will just ride up on a hypoallergenic horse and fix all our problems? Ah, at last, a savior! How wonderful! How inspiring! How romantic!

And how impossible.

I call this "Searching for your Missing Piece."

SEARCHING FOR YOUR MISSING PIECE

I had a *total* crush on Jeremy.

He was a successful filmmaker, and I fervently admired his passion and commitment to his craft. He was also a decent cook and cute to boot.

But Jeremy turned out to be a shitty boyfriend. He was distracted, distant, and usually out of town. The sex wasn't even that good. And yet I couldn't get him out of my head! Jeremy was Rachel catnip.

And then Jeremy dumped me.

I felt as if my soul had been amputated. My heart turned into a hollow, burning hole in my chest. I was devastated. (You'll hear more about Jeremy in chapter nine when we talk about rejection.) What was going on? Why did I miss him so much?

With a little time and perspective, I came to understand that my desperate need to be with Jeremy wasn't really about Jeremy at all. I felt scared and crappy on the inside, and Jeremy's attention had been distracting me from my own bad feelings. When he paid attention to me, I felt validated and good about myself. When he ignored me, I was so busy chasing after his affection that I didn't have to deal with my own inner mess.

I wasn't dating Jeremy just because I liked him; I was dating him because I hoped he could fix me.

There is a big problem with the "I'll date you and you'll fix me" scenario: it assumes that we are dependent on someone else for our wholeness and happiness. When we think that someone else can fix our "Missing Piece," we are pretty much enslaving them to be our validation machines. When the relationship is going well, we feel amazing. When it's not going well, we feel horrible. And deep down, we have a small, festering, and irrational belief: we believe that if the relationship ends, we will die.

We've put ourselves on an emotional roller coaster.

Because I felt so dependent on Jeremy, I was afraid to let him go even when it was clear that the relationship wasn't working.

Because I was scared, I couldn't make the best decision for myself—or him—because of what I thought I would lose.

Staying with someone because of how they "make" us feel is a classic Missing Piece confusion. When we're in a Missing Piece confusion, our relationship becomes obligatory and dependent rather than free and truly loving.

When Jeremy dumped me, I did feel lost. But here's the thing: I already was lost.

His departure simply exposed the truth.

PERFECTLY IMPERFECT

The fact is that we all feel like we have a Missing Piece. At the core of our beings, we each have a fundamental sense of being incomplete, imperfect, unsafe, and unfinished. It's a feeling of being unworthy of love.

You know this feeling: it's the one you get when you feel like you have done something wrong. Maybe you had a fight with a friend, screwed up at work, or you just woke up feeling crappy. When we get this feeling, we scramble to cover it up. We search for stuff in the world (houses, cars, wealth, esteem, success) to make it go away. And when our cover-up job stops working, we're fast on the prowl again. We are constantly trying to fill the Missing Piece.

"Anyone who falls in love is searching for the missing pieces of themselves."
—Haruki Murakami

In romantic love, we use our relationships to cover up the Missing Piece. Like I did with Jeremy, we expect our partners to make the bad feelings go away. ("Tell me I'm pretty," "Commiserate with me," "Tell me you love me.") And they do. And it works.

For a while.

And then it stops working. Uh-oh. This must not be the right person, we think. Because according to the great Hollywood romance, the *right* person would make the Missing Piece feeling go away *forever*. So if this relationship isn't covering up my pain anymore, then it's got to be a bad fit. So we dump our faulty partner and find someone else. And hope that *they'll* be "the one."

But here's the secret that Hollywood keeps on the down low: that terrible feeling of uncertainty and imperfection isn't going to go anywhere. It will never be "solved" by Prince or Princess Charming—or anyone else.

Because it's an intrinsic part of your human condition.

Anava Mala is a fundamental human misperception that causes us to feel as if we are incomplete and imperfect. This misunderstanding makes us feel as if there is always something lacking, which we frequently try to fill with resources from the outside world. However, this feeling of lack is simply a part of being human. And it can only be addressed internally, by us.

Your Missing Piece can never be "fixed" by someone else! Eureka! Stop the presses! We can end the search! Yes, your partner may briefly cover up your bad feeling, but soon enough it's going to sneak up from the basement and—voila!—appear again. Inevitably. Because it's always there. And we are so used to calling this feeling a "problem" that we never actually just sit in how it feels.

The bottom line: finding "the one" is not going to make you happy. You will never be "cured" by romantic love—not even when your lover is the vampire Edward, Mr. Darcy, Ryan Gosling, or Theo James.

Lasting happiness can only come from the *inner* recognition of your own worthiness.

Ohhhhhh, my friends, I understand that you may be disappointed in what you just read. You may want to toss this book down. You're thinking, "That's crap. This is a dumb book. I thought this was going to help me date! Other people *do* make me happy and bring me joy. I deserve connection and love!"

Yes, I understand—and I agree with you! And we'll get there. But here's the sixty-four-thousand-dollar question that we have to ask ourselves before we start to tango with another person: are you looking for *love?* Or, are you just looking for someone *to fix your problem?*

It's time to stop selling ourselves short. It's time to stop mistaking *romance* for *love.*

ROMANCE VS. LOVE

Romance is delicious. It's the bloom on the rose, the icing on the cake. It's full of good nether region tingles and all sorts of fun fantasies. We should all enjoy the thrill of a first kiss and the giddiness of falling in love.

But romance isn't love. Romance thrives on mystery; it can only exist in the adventure of uncertainty. Love, on the other hand, is rooted in intimacy, which is the deep knowledge of another person. In a sense, romance and love are polar opposites; as you get to know someone better, their mystery is dispelled. Their flaws appear. This is usually about the time that we get mad at our partners and think about ending the relationship.

And right in that very sticky moment lies the opportunity for love.

Love lies in our willingness to know someone else deeply: flaws, farts, and all. But you can only see someone else for who they really are when you aren't busy using them as a human shield for your own bad feelings.

When you stop trying to fix your own Missing Piece with your romantic partner, then you can see your person for who they are. Instead of *needing* the relationship, you can *choose* the relationship. And if your partner has a bad day, your world doesn't fall apart. Because you don't need them to be a certain way for you to be okay.

This time, we're going to do dating differently. We're not going to settle for romance. We're going to go for love.

Rather than seek out partners to fill our Missing Pieces, let's seek out partners because we want to *more fully* express ourselves and *connect authentically* with another human being. Let's seek out partners in order to cultivate true intimacy and see them for who they are beyond our own needs. And when our own unfinished business gets exposed, let's treat it as a glorious opportunity for a little self-work rather than a pity party.

Yoga

From the root, "yuj," to yoke. Think of an ox, yoked to a plow in order to sow a field. When we practice **yoga**, we are using **yoga** as a tool to connect more deeply with ourselves.

When we have a stronger sense of who we are, then we can arrive in our relationship adventures from a place of strength, rather than desperation; open-handed, rather than grasping; centered, rather than needy.

In some ways, this wake-up call seems like a complete bummer. "What, you mean I can't just find someone to fix what's wrong with me?"

Well, yes, you can. And you will.

That person is you.

Sat-cit-ananda means "whole, free, blissful," which is a description of our true identity. Although our connection to our true nature is usually obscured by the limitations of our own understanding, through practice we can begin to uncover and experience our intrinsic wholeness for ourselves.

PRACTICES

Journal: Heart's Desire

For this exercise, write freely and give yourself permission to brainstorm. Stream of consciousness, baby. The less you think about it, the better!

- What are the essential traits you crave in your dream partner (sexy, kind, entrepreneurial, creative, safe, wealthy, musical, funny)?

Be honest: what do you **really** want? The more specific and quirky that you can be, the better. Don't be polite, be real. No one's watching; share what you really want—not what you think sounds good. For example, one of the random things on my list: "I want someone who can change a tire on my car ... I find that damn sexy."

Dating Practice: Self-Dating

For every date that you go on with another person, make one date for yourself that is at least a half hour. Put it in your calendar.

For your self-date, consider one of the traits that you selected above. Now, choose an activity that will empower you to create that skill or emotional experience for *yourself*. For example, if you're a closet artist, sign up for painting lessons, or pull out your guitar. If you feel financially insecure, sign up for a course that helps you to manage your money, or set aside time to work on your budget. If you are seeking someone successful, find a personal coach, work on your résumé, or do job research.

- After each self-date, journal or reflect briefly: how do you feel?

By taking responsibility for our self-development, we practice self-trust, self-reliance, and self-empowerment. While we can choose to seek out someone with these qualities, cultivating them for ourselves deepens our capacity to remain centered and anchored.

Meditation Practice: Awakening

We all have a Missing Piece feeling. But we've become so good at covering it up that we reflexively react before we even notice it. We drink the wine, eat the cookie, or call the friend before we give ourselves a chance to experience our feelings. This meditation is an opportunity to become friendlier with ourselves *just as we are.*

Don't worry if you've never meditated before; this simple meditation is the perfect way to practice creating space to come home to yourself.

How to find your meditation seat

Choose a position that allows your spine to be long and tall without effort. While we usually think of yogis sitting on a cushion or block on the floor, you can also sit on the edge of a chair. The most important part of your meditation seat is that are you able to keep your spine upright and tall without undue effort. (If sitting is hard on your back, you can also lie down on your back with your knees bent.) Choose a position that you can stay in relatively comfortably for five minutes. If something starts hurting partway through the meditation, then don't be a hero! It's okay to change your position so that your body is at ease.

Once you are seated, feel the anchor of your sitting bones connecting to the earth. The sitting bones are the two boney prominences at the bottom of your pelvis. Position your chest over your pelvis and your head over your chest so that your skeleton supports your body weight without undue effort. As your head floats toward the sky, release any unnecessary tension in your shoulders and neck. You may find it helpful take a few circular shoulder rolls or to yawn to release any tension in your neck and jaw. Draw your shoulders back slightly to open and broaden your chest. Place your hands on your thighs (face up for a sense of openness, or face down for a sense of grounding).

I recommend closing your eyes. If you find that closing your eyes is disconcerting or that you start to feel sleepy, then keep your eyes open and softly focused.

For each meditation exercise, you can set a timer (I recommend starting with five minutes) or sit for as long as you wish. After each meditation, open your eyes and take a few moments to transition back to the "real world" before leaving your seat.

- Find your meditation seat (as described above).

- Breathe and sense your body and your feelings.

- Do an "internal scan" where you focus on the physical sensation in different parts of your body.

- What physical sensations do you feel?

- What emotions do you feel?

- Distraction will be natural. As thoughts arise, gently return your attention to your breath and to your feelings.

Yoga Practice: Self-Connection

Use your yoga practice to connect with how you feel. If your practice were a reflection of self-love, would it be different? How can you use these poses to nourish your connection with yourself?

- Cat/Cow

- Child's pose

- Downward dog

Chapter 3
IDENTITY

To develop intimacy with someone else, we must first become intimate with ourselves. We must dive into that big, juicy, fundamental question:

"Who am I?"

Since we left the caves thousands of years ago, we have been puzzling over the mystery of our identity.

Who am I? And how can I—whoever "I" am—be *happier?*

Your core beliefs about your identity underlie everything about how you work, live, and love. So it's a good idea to step back occasionally and take a look under the hood. Think of yourself as a computer for a moment; investigating your identity is a bit like examining and updating your operating system.

Yogis have been obsessed with figuring out human nature for a few millennia, and they've come to a few helpful conclusions. Trying on their worldview can help us break free of habitual patterns, expand our understanding of who we are, and enter our relationships with less fear and more grace.

Who Am I?

"It's nice to meet you, too," I say to Lucas, settling into my chair at Starbucks. It's early in my dating adventures, and I feel nervous.

Lucas grins back. He is a put-together guy, dressed casually, toffee-colored hair and nice brown eyes. And he's cuter than his OkCupid picture, heaven forfend. Much cuter, actually, now that I take a look at him. Friendly smile, kind eyes. There's that weird little tickle in the back of my head, a buzzing attraction.

Don't be a weirdo, Rach. Do not *start being a weirdo.*

"So ..." he says, "tell me something about yourself."

"Well ..." I say, "that's an open question!"

"It's a fresh start," he says grandly, "the floor is open!"

"Okay, well, then." I nod, take a breath, and smile in a way that might appear modestly captivating. "I'm a yoga teacher. Or rather, I'm the director of Teachers' College for YYoga. So I run all their teacher training programs, and I created their 200 hour ... that's the program that trains teachers to teach." I frown. Why am I trying to sound impressive?

I change tack. "Before I came to Vancouver, I lived in New York City, where I was an actor. Theater" I hastily specify, "not film. The stage." Uh-oh, do I sound like a snob? I think I sound like a snob. "I mean, I love film," I say very clearly, "but I was classically trained for the theater. The thea-TAH, ha ha. Mostly Shakespeare."

Oh, God, it was just getting worse.

I backtrack again. "Um, okay, so I wasn't so great at film, actually, I was always overacting. Too much of a ham, I guess. Hammy Rachel. Hammy hamster. Hammo-rific."

Rach, you're now being a weirdo. It's officially time to stop talking. Stop. Talking.

"So there we are. Me in a nutshell. A ham sandwich. Um. Ta-da." I try to hide in my chair. "Uh, and who are you?"

When I started dating, I began to realize that my knee jerk reaction when I'm asked to describe myself is to rattle off all the stuff that I think sounds good. I want the other person to like me, so out pours a giddy monologue of "impressive Rachel" talking points.

Naturally, in my monologues, I conveniently leave out all the other stuff that I don't like about myself so much.

That kind of intro would sound a bit different.

"Hi Lucas, damn, you're cute! Whooo-weee! Mama would approve of you. Well, about me, to be honest, I'm pretty anxious and absent-minded. I lose my car keys all the time. My car is dented because I keep running into stationary poles in parking garages. I'm very loving, but I have a really hard time dealing with anger and I can be a workaholic. I leave all the kitchen cabinet doors open when I cook, I tear my fingernails off as a cheap manicure, and I am profoundly hopeless with my hair. I had a really crappy divorce and then stayed in a relationship with a guy who didn't want kids for a really long time! I practice yoga so that I don't lose my mind or become a total head case. How's your latte?"

Even if I could encapsulate all of my behavior—good and bad—and somehow transmit it via Vulcan mindmeld to Lucas, would *that* have let him see the real me? Would that describe *who I am?*

Am I the sum total of my accomplishments, actions, and behavior? Or am I something more?

IGNORANCE

According to yoga, we suffer from a deep confusion: we believe that we *are* the stuff in our heads.

- "I'm a yoga teacher."

- "I love education."

- "I was an actor."

- "I love big cities."

Not only do we buy into the idea that we are defined by our thoughts, but we also believe that we are defined by our *feelings*, which can lead to a gigantic roller coaster ride of emotions.

- "I'm sad."

- "I suck."

- "I'm amazing!"

- "I'm the most horrible person ever."

As we walk around in the world, we are constantly identifying ourselves with all the noise crackling between our ears. I call this noise our "hamsters." Our thoughts and feelings are like crazy hamsters, racing around after every distraction and running on their hamster wheels. Unfortunately, they're dragging our sense of self along with them.

Avidya means "ignorance," or literally, "non-seeing." *Avidya* is the fundamental mistake we make in assuming that we are defined by the changing thoughts in our heads. According to yogic wisdom, we are not just our minds; we are actually the Presence who is *observing* our experience. Tapping into our true identity allows us to find more steadiness and self-reliance in a constantly changing world.

While our thoughts and feelings are an integral part of our human experience, identifying with them exclusively is a one-way ticket to suffering. We will be constantly adrift because our thoughts and feelings are always changing. Our happy sense of self will be shattered with one bad experience or an ill-spoken word. Getting fired from our job destroys our sense of pride in our competency. A fight with a loved one unmoors our sense of safety.

When I moved from New York City to British Columbia, my life was upended. Before the move, I had been an actor, a teacher, and a New Yorker. I felt incredibly proud of my association with the city as if I owned a piece of its glamour simply by living there.

When I arrived in Vancouver, all of the landmarks that I had been using to define myself were gone: I wasn't working, I had no history, no one knew me, and I was living in a city and a country that were unfamiliar. My husband, who could have been an anchor, disappeared suddenly into his alcohol addiction. My new marriage foundered. I completely fell apart.

During this time, I became painfully aware of how much my inner sense of self was anchored to the stuff outside of me. When those external landmarks disappeared, I felt lost. As it turns out, I had very little inner sense of self to rely on.

Ultimately, the external world can never give us stability.

But here's the root of our confusion: it's not supposed to.

REALITY

The nature of the universe is to change. Stars are born, they live, and they die. Tides move. Mountains crumble. Change is intrinsic to the fabric of life.

Prakriti is "Mother Nature" and encompasses the universe that is sensible (that is, that can be experienced through our five senses: sight, taste, touch, sound, smell). Mother Nature is composed of the elements: earth, air, fire, water, and space. It is the nature of all these elements to change. Everything in the world—the seasons, the tides, the phases of the moon, the beating of our heart—is subject to a beginning, middle, and end. Despite our attempts to fix it or control it, everything in the realm of *prakriti* is temporary.

There's only one problem: **our minds hate change**.

The mind wants the external world to be knowable, static, and permanent. Because uncertainty feels so scary, we spend a lot of time trying to control our environment and make the outer world behave in a way that we like. We are control freaks, scrambling for a foothold. It's like trying to make a fort on a rockslide: ultimately, it just won't work.

The *gunas* are "the qualities of nature." The three *gunas* describe the qualities of movement inherent in the material world. *Rajas* is quick and light, *tamas* is heavy and full of inertia, and *sattva* is luminous and balanced. All of Mother Nature is constantly moving and changing according to the influence of these qualities. In other words, everything is either speeding up, slowing down, or balancing ... until it changes.

Usually, our world doesn't change all at once. If we lose our job, we still have our marriage. Or if we change cities, we still have our work.

But have you ever been through a period when several pillars of your life became unmoored at the same time? You may have felt "lost" and not known "who you were." You may have felt groundless, anxious, and untethered.

During my move, I uprooted many pillars of my life at the same time. New country, new coast, new marriage, new home, no job, no friends, and no stuff.

No wonder I felt so unstable!

Despite our anxiety, these transitions can also be a gift because they reveal how much we rely on the external world for a sense of ourselves. While it can be painful at the time, these transition times help us realize that the external world does not define who we are. When everything falls apart, we have the opportunity to experience the Reality of the universe, which is that nothing is truly permanent. And—if we can soften to the experience—these moments offer a portal through which we can connect to something within us that is deeper.

"Only to the extent that we expose ourselves over and over to annihilation can that which is indestructible be found in us."
—Pema Chödrön

Because there is something that is stable, and permanent, and unchanging. And that's the Real You.

THE BIG SELF

Remember the movie *The Matrix?*

In the story, Neo's true self was trapped inside a pink tank of goo. However, even though he was stuck in a tank, he was hooked up to a virtual reality machine that made him think he was living a normal life in a computer-generated world called "The Matrix."

Although we may not be roped into a gestation tank full of pink goo like Neo, the way our minds work is not so different.

Like Neo, we are continually participating in the ultimate virtual reality game. However, we experience this virtual reality through an avatar called "you."

From the moment that you are born, everything that you sense, fear, and desire is perceived through a human suit that has five senses. Through your days and nights, you ride the roller coaster adventure of this virtual reality world. Your character goes to work, goes on dates, and meets with friends. Through your avatar, you experience the delights—and challenges—of the world. You can think of your avatar as your "Little Self."

But you are not the character in the movie. You are the Presence that is watching the movie. This Presence is your "Big Self." In our *Matrix* metaphor, your "Big Self" is the real Neo in the tank, watching the Little Neo have adventures in the Matrix.

When I moved to Vancouver, my Little Self was on a remarkable adventure. Everything in the world was changing for my avatar. I felt all the pain, loss, and loneliness of the main character's drama. And yet the Presence watching my experience was unchanged. My Big Self was there—unharmed—through all the drama of my life. However, I was so wrapped up in the experience that I often forgot that I was the Presence watching the story rather than the avatar.

When we begin to experience our Presence, we can step back and recognize that the movie isn't Reality. No matter what turmoil and change are happening in our lives, our Big Self is ultimately okay.

Think about it for a moment. Are you the same you that you were five years ago?

Well, in some ways, no. Certainly you have learned new skills, had new adventures, and perhaps changed the external trappings of your life. But is the same *you* looking out of your eyes? How about ten years ago, or twenty? Is the same *you* looking out of your eyes now as was looking out of your eyes when you were a child?

Yes.

Beneath all the change happening in the external world, there is something fundamentally unchanging in *you*. However, we're usually so busy believing all our thoughts and our feelings that we miss the opportunity to sit in this deeper, unchanging Presence.

Purusha

According to yoga philosophy, **purusha** is your true, unchanging Big Self. You can choose whatever word you like for it: consciousness, soul, higher self, absolute, or God. I'll refer to **purusha** as your Big Self, or Presence. Unlike **prakriti** (Mother Nature), **purusha** does not change or shift but is eternal and steady. Although we get confused and think that we are the stuff in our heads (which is in the realm of **prakriti**), we are actually **purusha**. We are Presence.

Can you recall a moment where the movie in your head has gone silent? Suddenly, the relentless mind hamsters stopped running around, and there you were: present, aware, being.

You may have even had a momentary recognition of how deeply you were connected with everything around you.

Many of us have experienced this wondrous awareness in savasana (corpse pose) or after meditation. In fact, this calm steadiness is often why we come back to our mats again and again. A Big Self moment can also arise spontaneously: walking through a forest, sitting with a loved one, or enjoying a sunset.

When we arrive in our Big Self, we experience that the moment is *now*, there is nowhere else to get to, and nothing better is around the corner.

This is yoga.

While we often associate yoga with practicing poses, the deeper goal of yoga is stilling the mind so that we can experience Presence. Physical movement has only been a part of the yoga tradition for a few hundred years. These poses are simply tools that help to support an awareness of the Big Self.

Usually, a Big Self moment will only last a moment or two before our thoughts rush back in and hurry us on to our day, agendas, fears, and obligations. The hamsters start running again! Our yoga practice is a tool that helps us to experience this connection to our essential self with more consistency.

Yoga Citta Vrtti Nirodhah

"Yoga is the restraint of the fluctuation of the mindstuff."
—Yoga Sutra

The *Yoga Sutra* is a compilation of yoga philosophy written by a sage named Patañjali about two thousand years ago. When we quiet the voices in our heads, we stop misidentifying our true self with all our mind chatter. When we stop identifying with the mind, we realize that we are already whole, already complete. The answer to our perpetual cravings for safety isn't outside; it's inside. When the mind stops racing, we discover that *we* are the answer that we have been waiting for.

When the stories in our head pause, we have a moment of clarity where we realize that we are not the incessant thoughts that are running through our mind. We are more than our "story." We are the Big Self or witness that lies behind our thoughts. We are the Presence watching the great virtual reality show with love, patience, and kindness.

"Go inside. Fall in love. Stay there."
–Rumi

As we cultivate our capacity to restrain our relentless thoughts and connect with our Presence, we become less dependent on the external world. We don't feel as compelled to defend our identity ("I am a teacher," "I am a happy person," "I am a Democrat," "I am single") because we recognize that these labels are temporary and can't possibly summarize the totality of who we really are.

When we experience Presence, we experience our intrinsic "okayness." We recognize that the fluctuations of the world, our minds, and our feelings will continue to rock and roll, and we are still safe, happy, and free.

Tat Tvam Asi

The Upanishads are stories and practices from about three thousand years ago, when yoga practitioners entered deeply meditative states seeking wisdom. One of the great wisdom sayings from the **Chandogya Upanishad** is **"Tat Tvam Asi,"** or "That thou art." In other words, you are the very essence that you are seeking.

"So ..." he says, "tell me something about yourself."

"Well, Lucas, I'm an eternal being of light, love, and Presence that is currently experiencing the material world in a changing human form. Mmmmm, wow Starbucks makes a great Americano! And you?"

Yeah, no ... I'm not going to say this.

Well, at least not on a first date.

While it's all well and good to realize that our Big Self is a transcendental Presence that defies material existence, we also live and work (and date) in the real world. We need our senses, egos, bodies, and minds to move through life.

As real-world yogis, our work is to stay connected to the Big Self while we use our Little Self to get around. This is called *mindfulness*, or as I call it, *practicing the pause.*

Mindfulness is the practice of staying connected to our Big Self as we negotiate the marvelous complexity of the world. When we practice the pause, we step back from the chaos of our mind hamsters and return to Presence.

Connecting to the Big Self doesn't mean that we don't get to enjoy all the juiciness of our senses. Quite the contrary! When we are able to stay connected to our Big Self in the present moment, then we can experience our mind and our emotions without being ruled or overwhelmed by them. We can enjoy the richness and adventure of our human experience without losing our center. In fact, we will be able to enjoy a richer, lusher, and more vibrant experience because we won't be as scared that we can really be hurt.

DATING

Dating is the perfect playing ground for practicing mindfulness because of the uncertainty. The terrible, exciting uncertainty.

In our day-to-day lives, we usually pretend that we can control the world. We have habitual routines that give us a sense of steadiness, and we can forget to stay connected to the Big Self.

When we go out on a date, we disrupt our routines and wake up. We can't possibly know how anything is going to go because we're meeting a perfect stranger! During a date, the fundamental uncertainty and shiftiness of the world are exposed. And in the midst of all that chaos, we can practice returning to the fundamental and unshakable ground of our Big Self.

Through staying connected to the Big Self, we can play the game of dating—and life—with less fear and more possibility.

PRACTICES

Journal: Who Am I?

- Write a list of the adjectives that you often use to describe yourself.

- How would your friends describe you?

- Are these words always accurate?

- If you are not these words, are you still *you?*

Reflection: Who Am I?

- Looking back at your life, can you think of a time when "you" have not been you?

- Who was looking out of your eyes five years ago?

- Who was looking out of your eyes ten years ago?

- Who was looking out of your eyes when you were a child?

Dating Practice: Bring Your Soul Along

- As you introduce yourself to your date, notice what you say. Notice what your date says. Reflect upon how you both are defining yourselves—and why.

- During your date, periodically take a few moments to breathe and clear your mind. Can you sit in the open space of possibility?

Meditation Practice: Finding Presence

Our solution is not outside but within.

Set a timer for five minutes, or sit as long as you wish.

- Find your meditation seat (see chapter two for more detailed instructions if needed).

- Focus on your breath.

- As the thoughts arise, acknowledge them. Then allow them to fall away. Notice the space between your thoughts.

- Who is watching your thoughts?

- Sit in the space of Presence.

Yoga Practice: Inward Looking

- Forward fold

Close your eyes. Either hold on to opposite arms or bring your fingertips to your shins or the floor. Close your eyes, sense your body, and take five deep breaths.

Chapter 4
EXPRESSION

"What's Tinder?" I ask.

"Where have you been?" My roommate stares at me. "It's, you know, the swiping thing," she says, making a slashing finger gesture. "You swipe right for 'yes,' or left for 'no.'"

"The swiping thing?"

My roommate sighs. "Yes, you know, you swipe right or left on their profile pic. If you both swipe right, then it's a match and then you can chat."

"You base it on a picture?" I wrinkle my nose. "Wow, that sounds superficial."

My roommate rolls her eyes. "Welcome to this century, Lava Life."

Lava Life was an online dating site from the 1990's. It was not considered cool.

"You start by making an online profile," she says. "C'mon, pull out your phone."

"Now?" I hedge.

"You said you wanted something to be different. So now you have to do something different." She grabs my phone. "First stop: Tinder."

"Oh, God."

CONSCIOUSNESS

What could Tinder possibly have to do with yoga? Hold on to your hats, my friends, because you are about to find out. In fact, you're going to see how Tinder is actually a powerful vessel for evolving your personal human potential.

It's just cleverly disguised as a dating app.

While your fundamental nature is pure, unchanging awareness (your Big Self, as discussed in chapter three), you also have the opportunity to be embodied in a human form (your Little Self) that is living in the material world (*prakriti*). Like Neo from The *Matrix*, you are in a virtual reality game called "Being a human being on planet Earth." And within your little human suit, your soul is having a grand adventure, filled with drama, emotions, victories, and defeats.

While it may be a game, it is a serious game. And it matters how you play.

While some schools of yoga do encourage practitioners to retreat from the world to stay only in the Big Self, modern yoga is influenced by the lineage of tantra. In tantra, playing the game is an important part of our soul's experience. (More on this in chapter eleven, when we talk about sex, wheeee!)

We—humans—have a rare quality on this planet: consciousness.

By consciousness, I am referring to your remarkable ability to be mindful and reflective. Unlike your cat, your dog, or your favorite guinea pig, you have the ability to stop, take a breath, and decide what you want to do. And with every choice that you make, you create and reveal who you are.

Let's take that again. Read it slowly:

With every choice that you make, you create and reveal who you are.

Lila (divine play) describes the ultimate play of the universe, which has been set into motion so that the universe can express and reveal itself in all of its diversity. Think of the singularity before the Big Bang: everything in the universe was encapsulated in a pure point of energy-matter-consciousness. As soon as the Big Bang happened, the universe expanded and began to cool. As the universe cooled, the myriad potential forms within that original singularity began to be expressed. The material world is actually the fabric of Universal Consciousness, expressing itself through divine play. And that includes you.

We are creating the world—and the collective identity of humanity—with *every single action that we take*. And through our actions, we decide which qualities we want to see expressed and upheld in the world. Are you lamenting the lack of compassion in the world? Act more compassionately! Do you want to see more bravery in the world? Step into your own fear. Do you want the world to have more love? Be more loving.

"Life isn't about finding yourself. Life is about creating yourself."
—Anonymous

You are not separate from the seething, glorious world: you are an intrinsic part of it. You *are* the very fabric of the universe. Everything that you do—large or small—creates the world as you go. Each positive step that you take forward propels humanity toward a better version of itself.

"If we could change ourselves, the tendencies in the world would also change."
—Gandhi's statement invites us to follow our highest vision and embody our best self—regardless of circumstance

However, we often forget that we are mighty architects of creation. We get tired, cranky, distracted, and it's easy to be reactive. We feel irrelevant and fall into the trap of thinking, "What's the point?" Remaining mindful takes vigilance.

"Whatever you do will be insignificant, but it is very important that you do it."
—Gandhi

Small daily acts matter. We usually know that we are going astray when we hear a little voice chirp in our ear: "You don't need the donut," "Call your mother," or "Don't get mad; it's not the Starbucks barista's fault." Sometimes we act out and feel our consciences twinge with regret.

We don't need to blame ourselves for our habits or reactive tendencies. We are not always capable of keeping our Big Self in the driver's seat. However, our work is to do our best to stay awake and remember our capacity for mindful self-creation.

Which is why we have to practice.

Iccha Shakti is the divine creative urge for self-expression. Everything in the universe is in a state of expressing itself and its nature. Because we are a part of the universe, we can participate in this dance by consciously choosing our own self-expression, simply for the joy of being who we really are.

You can start with your online dating profile.

When you write your profile description or upload a photo, you are expressing who you are in the world. Through words and images, you are creating (and it is a creative act!) your identity. So why not choose to put up a profile that shares your authentic, best self?

There are two parts to this process: *authenticity* and *elevation*.

The first part of this process involves *authenticity*. You do not need to change your age, height, and weight because you think that you need to be younger, taller, or thinner. On the contrary. Being your best self means being *you*. If you are passionate about *Star Trek* or get giddy over LEGO, then say so. Love animals and the environment? Put it in. Family-focused? Bam. Your profile is the time to share who you really are.

Now, not everyone will agree with this. They'll say, "No, Greta, don't post a picture of your trip to LEGOLAND because you may turn some guys off. Post that photo where you look sexy and amazing in that cocktail dress."

I say bullshit. Don't post a photo of yourself in a cocktail dress unless you get dreamy over Vera Wang. Sharing your authentic self will feel vulnerable. But hiding does not serve you. Not everyone likes LEGO, and that's okay. And someone who doesn't appreciate your LEGO passion isn't going to be your person, anyway, right?

Dig deep, friends. It's time to let go of shame and fear! It's time to stop editing and start sharing. When you are your best, you are not conforming to an artificial standard of what you think other people will like, but rather you are acting from a place of integrity that reflects your wonderful, unique self.

The second part of this process is *elevation*.

Creating an online profile is a chance to *practice the pause* and consider how you want to be in the world.

What does "being your *best* self" mean to you? What values do you want to express in the world? Who do you aspire to be?

- Kind

- Patient

- Adventurous

- Fun

- Courageous

- Loyal

Your "best self" is your inner vision for who you are, a north star that can guide and govern your behavior and your choices. It is a vision that will evolve over time.

Creating your profile is not a casual endeavor. This is an opportunity to choose how you want to show up in the world and in your relationships. In taking the time to reflect upon your "best self," you will begin to get a richer and more integrated sense of your own personal values. You will be choosing how you want to participate in the world, and in the great divine play of universal creation.

Creating your Tinder profile is just the start. Once you've set your vision, then it's time to *live* your best self.

OBJECTIFICATION

"OMG, can you believe this one?" I say to my roommate. "His only picture was clearly taken at his wedding and his wife's face is blacked out."

"God! Ew!" she exclaims, swiping left on Tinder. "Don't they know anything?"

"Seriously!" I say. "And this one has a picture of his boat and his house, but no picture of him. Where is his self-respect?" I continue swiping. "This one has the spelling of a fifth grader ..." Swipe. "And this one, oh my God, the only picture is taken from about sixty feet, and he wants to have his first date 'at his house?' How does that not sound like a serial killer?"

I pause and stop.

"Ummmm." My forehead crinkles. "Wait a minute. Have I become too ... judgmental?"

"God, no." She waves her hand. "I scan the height, the job, the location. If those don't match up, I swipe left."

"But seriously," I tug her attention off her iPad. "Is doing this making us more, well, callous?"

She pauses, suddenly thoughtful.

"Yeah, I know what you mean," she finally sighs. "But who has time to give everyone a chance?"

Correspondence on dating sites can be overwhelming. It's a freaking full-time job. On Tinder, you may blast through fifty profiles in three minutes. On sites like OkCupid, eHarmony, Match.com, and Plenty of Fish, you could get upwards of ten connections per day. To cope with all the information, we become desensitized to the fact that there is a human being on the other end of the Wi-Fi. It is all too easy to ignore messages in the inbox.

Delete, delete, delete. Block. Delete.

"They'll get the message," we think.

And yes, they probably will. After a few days, or a week.

The conversation with my girlfriend was a wake-up call: I was starting to treat other people like video game characters.

"About one in ten," wrote one of the men with whom I'd corresponded. "That's about how often I get a response from a woman I've written to."

One of the qualities that I want to embody is compassion. And I certainly wasn't being compassionate when I was treating other people like Halo avatars.

I made a resolution: I would respond to every email and message I received, even when the email was from "MrMeatTube101," "SirBeerGogglesU," and "AgedStallion779."

> "Thanks for getting in touch. I enjoyed reading your profile. While I don't think that we are a great match, I appreciate your time and interest. Good luck in your search."

Small acts matter.

If I wanted to uphold the value of compassion, then I needed to treat each person who reached out to me with respect. Even when the only thing they wrote was, "hey gurrrl."

Who do you want to be? And how can your online interactions reflect your values?

Yoga philosophy offers guidelines for interacting with the world with integrity. The first guideline, *ahimsa*, is nonviolence, or compassion. All subsequent guidelines are built on its benevolent and powerful foundation.

The **yamas** are one of the eight "limbs" of yoga as described by Patañjali in the **Yoga Sutra**. The five yamas are guidelines for interacting ethically with the external world. They are nonviolence, truthfulness, non-grasping, non-stealing, and celibacy. (We'll talk about the truth in chapter eight and celibacy in chapter eleven.) These five guidelines are considered "great vows" that need to be upheld regardless of circumstance. In other words, no excuses. Adhering to these principles helps you keep your Big Self in the driver's seat.

Ahimsa

The first guideline for conduct, **ahimsa** means nonviolence or non-harming. However, **ahimsa** is not necessarily passive or complacent. Nonviolence may be fierce and active.

If you also value compassion, try this challenge: respond to every communication that you receive. Your response doesn't have to be lengthy; even a brief exchange can acknowledge someone else as a person. Make it easy on yourself and use copy/paste. Responding may seem like a small gesture, but small gestures form the fabric of human interaction.

Most importantly, making a practice of responding to these inquiries will shift the way that *you* feel.

When we take the time to see the humanity in each person and to treat them with care and respect, then we become more sensitive to our connection to all of the people around us—whether we're connecting with them through email, text, on the phone, or even face to face.

We are upholding the values of our Big Self.

PRACTICE THE PAUSE

While our photos and texts reveal who we are in the digital world, our *actions and speech* create and reveal who we are *in the real world.* How you choose to act every day in your relationships—with your family, at your jobs, or with strangers on a coffee date—is a direct expression of who you are and *who you want to be.* In short, every interaction that you have is an opportunity to uphold and embody your values in the world, in real time.

Ahamkara is "ego," or the "I-maker," that helps us to distinguish ourselves from the world around us. ("I am happy, I am sad, I am a good person, I am an architect, I am a yogi, I am a mother," etc.) We need our ego to make our way through the world. The question is, who do we want this "I" to be?

In your online profile, you are defaulting to habit when you only post the photos that make you look hot or are easy to access in your camera roll.

In life, you default when you let the *habit* of who you have been dictate who you are *becoming.*

Our first step in elevating our own expression is to *practice the* pause *so that we can choose who we want to be.* While creating your online profile was an opportunity to create a vision for who you are in the world, arriving at your date is an opportunity to *practice* bringing that vision to life.

"Mindfulness practice means that we commit fully in each moment to be present; inviting ourselves to interface with this moment in full awareness, with the intention to embody as best we can an orientation of calmness, mindfulness, and equanimity right here and right now."
—Jon Kabat-Zinn, *Wherever You Go, There You Are*

MY FIRST TINDER DATE

My first date was pretty much an autopilot disaster.

"Oh God, oh God," I'm thinking. "Please let me recognize him from his picture. Just please let me recognize him. Please don't let me be staring at him awkwardly right now or make an overture to the wrong person. Pleeeease."

I'm sandwiched into the foyer of a crowded and trendy brunch spot, waiting for my first-ever online date (from Tinder!) to show up. I've dressed in jeans (which feels positively formal since I usually live in my Dharma Bums leggings), and I've even combed my hair. Big effort. My stomach is churning.

Ethan walks in the door. I recognize him. Thank God. He actually looks like his picture. I've heard people don't usually look like their pictures. But he does.

"Uh, hey," he says and smiles. He's tall and has a cute gap between his two front teeth.

"Hi, uh. Nice to ... uh, hey!" Awkward hug. I bite my tongue from saying, "Nice to meet you," advertising "FIRST

DATE" in neon letters to the lounging hipsters who no doubt smell Tinder all over this.

The hostess is perky. "Come this way, I can seat you now that you're both here."

We get ourselves sorted, take control of the menus (I'm clumsy with mine; it feels like an ungainly, fluttering bird), and manage to order.

"So, um, where are you from?" I venture.

He speaks and eats slowly, as if he's taking the measure of everything in his mouth. I'll find out later that this is how Ethan moves in the world: slowly, carefully, and with deliberate intent. He swallows. "Folks live back east. Sister, too. You?"

"Oh wow. East, uh, me too. Born in good ol' New Hampshire, you know the uh, live free or die state! Yep, we've got some fight." My face feels weird. I realize I'm smiling really widely. I try to stop it, but I can't. It's alarming. Kind of like the Joker in Batman. Maybe talking will fix this problem.

"Then I was in New York City for about a decade, oh goodness!" (Goodness?) "A decade, whoa! That makes me sound old, ha ha, well, San Francisco for a few years, too, at school, then New York again, but you know, I counted that in the decade there already, not thirteen years, but ten all told ..."

I start to have an out of body experience. Where was this horrific, vomitus chattiness coming from? Poor Ethan, barely a word out and here I was submerging him in a horrible torrent of small talk. I try to stop talking, but it's as if a dam has been released and the water just won't stop. Apparently, I become a rabidly chipper one-sided conversationalist when I get uncomfortable.

Who knew?

THE GIFT OF SELF-CONSCIOUSNESS

During a date, we are painfully aware and pinned to the present moment. And in our discomfort, we can either fall back onto our protective habits, or we can *practice the pause*, take a breath, and make a choice about how we want to act.

While I'd experienced "awareness" before on the yoga mat, dating became an opportunity to put this pause into practice in the good company of others. Dating is the perfect place to practice mindfulness because we're usually a little freaked out. The world becomes more vivid. Time slows down.

And in this slightly freaked out space, we have a choice. We can either run on autopilot by defaulting back to all our comfortable control strategies, or we can *practice the pause* and choose how we want to show up, moment by moment.

When you start to put yourself out there on Tinder or Plenty of Fish, you may have a lot of first dates. Each one is an opportunity to put yourself back in the fire of not knowing. To start with a blank canvas and see what you will create.

After Ethan, I went on a lot of first dates.

While I still wanted to fill the silence with my babbling, I started practicing the pause and waiting. At first, allowing for silence felt interminable! I squirmed, I blushed, I literally had to bite my tongue. But as I practiced, I became more comfortable staying in the void. And when I did, often my date would find something interesting to say that would take the conversation in a marvelous and unexpected direction.

By practicing the pause, I came one step closer to being the good listener that I want to be. Not just in dating, but in all my relationships.

By questioning our default patterns, we become artists of self-creation. Our actions become the colors that we use to create the masterpiece of our lives.

*"Practice does not make **perfect**. Only **perfect practice** makes perfect."*
—Vince Lombardi

Because dating usually makes us self-conscious, it's the perfect time to both witness and transform our habits. Each and every time we show up for a coffee date, we can take a breath and treat it as a twenty-minute practice. Do we want to practice compassion, honesty, good listening—even when we feel like our feet are in the fire? Here is an opportunity to step up our game and consciously embody our best vision for ourselves.

Here's the thing:

We are not showing up as our best selves to make a great impression or to wow our dates. We're showing up as our best selves *for us*. Because we have a vision for who we want to be, and how we want to uphold ourselves in the world.

Return, moment by moment, to the extraordinary power of your own ability to choose who you want to be. Your small daily acts will change the world. You will inspire others. We will all shine more brightly.

And most importantly, you'll align your actions with who you want to be.

PRACTICES

Journal: Expression

Brainstorm who you are and who you aspire to be.

- During which activities do you feel the most alive, the most vibrant, the most "you"?

- Write down ten positive adjectives that describe who you are now.

- Write down ten negative adjectives that describe how you are now.

- Write down ten adjectives that describe who you want to be.

- What kind of beauty/handsome devil are you (circle as many as apply):

Women: Statuesque / elegant / athletic / cute / lovely / attractive / luscious / firebolt / rebel / hippy / earth mother / quirky / elfin / rubenesque / sensual / vibrant / quiet / subtle / vivacious / delicate / create your own

Men: Handsome / cute / athletic / attractive / strong / robust / wiry / passionate / generous / energetic / powerful / mystical / sensitive / mellow / considerate / solid / papa bear / earthy / create your own

Bonus Exercise: we usually develop our "negative" attributes for a very good reason. For example, my tendency to "bottle up my feelings" was a strategy for making sure I kept the peace. However, as adults, these old ways of being may be outdated and we may now have better tools that can accomplish the same result.

Choose one of the negative adjectives on your list. Write that adjective a love letter to thank it for its service and recognize its good intentions. By acknowledging the origin of our coping strategies, we can begin to let them go and replace them with something better.

Journal: Mission

Start to craft a personal mission statement for your life. A mission statement is an anchor that helps us stay rooted when the winds of life blow. It doesn't have to be grandiose; it can be very simple. Don't worry: your first draft does not have to be perfect. In fact, your mission will change and evolve over time.

- Try a free-writing exercise where you do a stream of consciousness and see what comes out. "My life's purpose is ..."

- Ask your trusted friends what they see as your best qualities and most poignant challenges.

- Reflect on what activities and interests have always called to you.

Dating Practice: Expression

- Set aside time to consciously choose how you want to express yourself on social media and online dating sites. Choose photos that express who you really are when you are doing something you love, rather than photos that you think "look good."

- On your dates, how do you arrive? Which part of yourself are you bringing forward?

  - o Consider the tangible: what do you want to wear? What clothing represents you? Do you love using makeup, perfume, cologne?

  - o Consider the less tangible: what kind of energy do you want to arrive with? Can you schedule your day to give yourself the time to transition to this state? For example, if you want to feel grounded, consider doing something for yourself before you arrive on the date that helps you feel connected and solid (yoga, perhaps?).

Dating Practice: Compassion

- Respond to every message rather than ignore communication. Even if it's just to say, "Thanks for your interest, I don't think we're a good match," take the time to acknowledge the other person as someone worthy of respect.

Meditation Practice: Cultivating Mindfulness

- Find your meditation seat (see chapter two for more detailed instructions if needed).

- Begin to observe the movement of your breath.

- Count your inhalations (1, 2, 3 ...)

- When your mind wanders off the numbers, then restart at 1.

- When you fall off course, compassionately bring yourself back to attention without judgment.

Yoga Practice: Expression

- Sun salutations

Sun salutations are infinitely varied! Each sun salutation can be different. As you practice, explore all the ways that you can express your feelings in these movements. Take your arms wide, take your arms forward, move quickly, move deliciously slowly. What feels good in each moment?

In your practice this week, express your best self.

What this means:

- Be honest with yourself in your practice: is this your personal best expression of the pose in this moment?

- Continually return to mindfulness during the practice. Our mind will naturally slip away. When you find yourself admiring your pedicure, return to the feeling of your body and your breath.

Chapter 5
CLARITY

My ex-boyfriend sent me an email to let me know that he was seeing someone.

A month after our six-year relationship ended.

I sit, staring stupidly at my computer, trying to register the polite words on the screen. *"I don't know how to come out and say it, so I guess I'll just tell you: I'm seeing someone."*

The flood of unexpected feelings is fast and hot. I am outraged, hurt, abandoned, destroyed. My mind spins with stories. Why couldn't he wait? Did our relationship mean so little to him? And who the hell is she?

He is with someone else.

He loves someone else.

And now, suddenly, I feel truly alone. The illusion that we were still somehow connected is broken.

As I start to cry over my keyboard, a surprising thought surfaces: "Well, I guess you weren't quite as over that as you thought, were you?"

REALITY BITES. AND WINS.

Reality checks are hard.

When the way that I want the world to be and the way that the world actually *is* collide, life does not feel good. My version of the way things *should* be is so much better. So when Reality (and we'll use capitalized "Reality" here to indicate that it's the real thing rather than the stories in our heads) finally knocks at my door, I want to fight defiantly for my version of events: "My ex should be mourning our breakup, not dating again so soon!"

We fight Reality constantly, burying our heads in the sand and practicing denial. "I shouldn't have gotten that parking ticket!" you might lament, even though you didn't feed the meter. "My bank balance should be higher," you may say, even though you took that delicious trip to Bali. We turn off the TV (or turn on the TV) to avoid dealing with what makes us uncomfortable. "I'm happier not knowing," you might declare, putting a big blindfold over your eyes.

But the problem is that the blindfold isn't hiding Reality; Reality is always there. The blindfold simply hides your own uncomfortable reaction to the truth. When you selectively ignore parts of the world, you are depriving yourself of the opportunity to be in the world as it actually is.

And ultimately, Reality will always win.

No matter how much we try to shove it down, deny it, or cover it with pretty blankies, Reality is our benevolent and relentless teacher.

My Reality? My ex-boyfriend was dating someone else. Full stop. No getting around it. The ties were cut; the relationship was over.

And even though I felt awful about it, knowing the truth put me more in touch with Reality. I had a fuller understanding of the truth of his life. And through witnessing my own reaction, I had a deeper understanding of my own feelings as well.

Reality is the stern mama bear who hugs us while growling the truth in our ears. Reality provides a mirror where we can experience our reactions and see who we are. And while Reality may be dishing out some tough love, it's love all the same.

WHAT'S REAL?

To understand our relationship with Reality, let's consider for a moment how much we can know about it.

Think about your five senses: sight, hearing, taste, touch, smell.

We can't perceive everything that's really out there because—quite literally—our senses are not wired to take it all in. For example, our sight is limited to perceiving wavelengths that are detectable only by the human eye; we can't see ultraviolet or infrared light, even though they surround us all the time. Similarly, we can't smell or hear the world anywhere near as well as our canine friends.

Manas

Sometimes called the "lower mind," *manas* pulls together the sensory information that we can perceive and compiles it to create our experience of the world. Through *manas*, we experience the environment of our virtual reality game.

And yet despite the limitations of our senses, we continue to believe that everything we perceive is the "truth."

Not only are we *physically* limited in our ability to perceive the world, but we are also limited by our mind's ability to consciously process the information as well. In a famous 1956 paper, psychologist George Miller proposed that two *million* bits of information come through our senses at any given moment.

Out of those two million bits, how many do you think that we are able to consciously perceive?

Seven, plus or minus two.

Take that in for a moment. That's **5–9** bits of information out of **two million**.

Humbling, no?

Samkhya philosophy is a sister philosophy of yoga that created a map to describe the human experience of Reality. According to *samkhya*, the elements (earth, air, water, fire, ether) are at the bottom of the map. The human mind perceives these elements through our senses. We put all this information together in our heads, which gets filtered through our ego, memory, and higher mind. The map of **samkhya** describes the limitations of human perception and invites us to keep an open space for possibility when we are deciding what is true.

The tiny amount of information that does manage to make it into our consciousness is then filtered by our egos, expectations, memories, desires, and fears. In other words, we tend to see what we want or expect to see, whether that means we're wearing rose-colored glasses or preparing for the worst. We filter out information that doesn't match our version of what we expect or want. Ask two people to describe a situation (or God forbid, a relationship), and the two narratives might be wildly different.

Before my ex-boyfriend emailed me, I had been assuming that he was still languishing over our failed relationship. Even though we had officially broken up, part of me wanted to hold on to the idea that he was continuing to love me from afar. His email exposed the distance between my assumptions and Reality.

You Say Tomato, I Say Tomahto

"Together or separate?" the waitress asks. She's so darn perky.

"Oh, we'll get separate checks," Ethan says as he peers up at the waitress from his glasses. Remember Ethan? My first Tinder date? I look down at my hands. Separate checks, huh. Well, that's a sign. Ethan is clearly not interested in dating. A guy who is interested in dating pays for the date, like a sign of intent. Some modern caveman version of: "I can provide for you and for our offspring; here is the brunch that I have hunted and killed."

I like Ethan a lot, but clearly this is going to be a friendship kind of thing. I pull out my credit card. Ah well. My first-ever online date was complete.

"I'll give you a call," he says.

"Great," I say. "Sure, I'd like that." And I would. He's a good conversationalist, an interesting guy, and super smart. So what if there's not a spark? Hug, hug, see you later.

Ethan and I start hanging out casually. We hit the art museum and see an interesting film at a festival. Ethan becomes a new member of my buddy circle.

"You know, I remember when we met," he says from the kitchen. "Who knew we'd be here now."

"Right? So crazy!" I call back from the living room. He's making popcorn while I scroll through movies to watch. "First dates are the worst. Figuring out the signals is so freakin' confusing." I pause the mouse over an old *Star Trek* movie. I'm such a nerd. "But *you* were totally clear at least."

"What do you mean?"

"Oh, you know: the whole check litmus test. If he pays, he's interested. If he's not, we split. I mean," I add hastily, "it all works out eventually, you know. I mean, I do start paying for things. But the first date? That's one of the basic signs. That's like, 101."

There's a long pause. A growing pause. An uncomfortable pause.

"Uh, no," Ethan says. "Uh, that's not how I do it. That's good to know."

My jaw drops. I suddenly realize that Ethan and I have been in living in two different Realities.

In Ethan's world, we have been dating for two weeks.

And I had had no idea.

"Don't believe everything you think."
—Anonymous

Understanding the limitations of our perceptions allows us to stay flexible about what we think is true. If we can recognize our tendencies to fix and solidify our version of the facts, then we can be more available to compassionately lean into the scary uncertainty that we don't actually know everything that is going on. Had I not been so assumptive about my version of Reality, I may have noticed sooner that Ethan and I weren't on the same page.

GETTING CLEAR: TRUE AND FALSE

If you recall from chapter three, yoga takes this view of the human mind:

- We have a lot of stuff in our heads.

- When we pause, we can stop identifying with all that stuff.

- Then we experience our Big Self.

- This is yoga.

Now, if we could just smack ourselves on the forehead at this point and "get it," we'd all reach enlightenment and could call it a day.

However, it usually takes more than that.

Our mind chatter isn't going to magically go away. Nor do we want it to. While we are living in our human virtual reality suit, we need our minds to drive cars, make enchiladas, sail boats, and—generally—live our lives. The mind is like a houseguest that won't leave. But since it's a houseguest that happens to make the food, pay the bills, and do all the chores, we're pretty happy to have it around. And while we're living together, we want to have a good relationship.

Part of your work as a yogi is to get friendlier with your mind so that it can properly do its job: be a magnificent tool for helping your soul to have an experience of itself and the world. When we recognize the limitation of our perceptions, then we can be more compassionate with ourselves and others. We can also stay open to the fact that Reality could be far different (and perhaps even better) than we thought.

TRUE PERCEPTION

The yoga tradition identifies a few different categories of "mind stuff" (*vrtti*) to help us recognize what's going on. Over the next few chapters, we'll take a look at these different kinds of mind stuff in order and get friendly with how they shape our Reality.

The first kind of mind stuff is called True Perception. True Perception is when our virtual reality game accurately reflects Reality. Or at least as much as it can. Although we can never be completely sure that we're correct, we are usually experiencing True Perception if one of the following conditions is met:

- I see my date steal some tableware. I perceive it directly.

- My best friend tells me that my date stole tableware. I have heard about it from someone I trust.

- I come back to the dining table, the tableware is gone, and I see it in his murse. I've made a sensible inference based on the available information.

Vrttis–Pramana

Vrttis are thought patterns, otherwise known as the "mind stuff". These are what I lovingly call our hamsters. Basically, it's the stuff in our heads. Understanding the different kinds of stuff in our heads helps us stay open to not believing everything that we think.

One of the thought patterns that we can experience is called "True Perception" (***pramana vrtti***). Perception is "true" (or accurate) when it is based on our direct experience, a trustworthy source, or sensible and consistent deduction.

Michael was a tall, handsome man in his mid-forties. We had exchanged a few pleasantries over Plenty of Fish before deciding to meet up for dinner near my work.

He was dressed smartly in standard business casual (for which he charmingly apologized, "Sorry to look so formal, straight from a work meeting!"). Since I'm a yoga teacher, I am impressed when someone isn't wearing spandex.

Michael had a steady, upper management job with an accounting company that he had worked with for nearly twenty years. He was a great listener, asked good questions, and seemed genuinely interested in my responses (which is not to be taken for granted!).

However, he seemed a bit too, well, straight and narrow for my tastes. Stable, centered, no surprises.

Having walked a not-so-straight path myself, I tend to connect with people who are a little off center. Michael, while charming and sweet, didn't seem like the kind of guy who would jaywalk, let alone break out a tin of kinky cocoa butter. However, he was a dreamboat: stable, handsome, and attentive. My mother would have loved him. So why was he single?

"Okay, are you just out of a relationship? Why are you online? What's the deal?" I ask bluntly.

He laughs. "Forthright, aren't you?"

I shrug. "Well, otherwise, what's the point? There are a lot of people out there who say they want a relationship, but they don't really want to commit. So they date a bunch of people but don't really want to settle down. Nothing wrong with that," I say quickly, "but not what I'm looking for."

"Ah," he says, "the Peter Pan syndrome."

"Yes, exactly. Never grow up."

"Right. They want to be intimate with different people, but they're not honest about it."

Something in his tone clicks for me, and I sit back. My eyes narrow. "Wait a second. So … tell me what you think about monogamy."

He is startled into laughter and puts his fork down. "Well, oh man. Yeah, you caught me. Um … okay." He blushes, just a little. "Usually this doesn't come out on a first meet, but … yeah. I don't think much of it."

"Don't like monogamy?"

"No, not really."

"But you do like being committed?"

"Yes. I enjoy commitment. I like loving relationships." He pauses. "I'm a polyamorist."

My eyes widen. Ah ha!

Like the reclusive unicorn, I had managed to find—and in the shape of a conservatively dressed, take-home-to-your-mama businessman, no less—a polyamorist. Someone who believes that you can love and be in a relationship with more than one person at the same time.

"Wow!" I am impressed. "Polyamorist!" Turns out my mother wouldn't have approved of Michael after all.

"Yes."

"You know, honestly," I say candidly, "I wouldn't have thought. You seem so straight-laced."

He is sincere. "It took me a long time to come to this decision, but it really does feel like the right thing for me. Allowing yourself to only love one person seems limited."

"Wellll," I clarify, and tilt my head, "I think you can love as many people as you like. I think it's the having sex with more than one person that gets people into trouble."

"But isn't sex part of intimacy?" he counters.

He's got me there. I consider his words. "Okay. I can see that. It makes sense in a certain way. I haven't gone down that road ... but I can see it." And I can. If you could just love people and not let boundaries or insecurities run the show, polyamory could make a lot of sense.

"How's the time management?" I ask. I barely have time for my cat. The logistics are boggling.

He smiles ruefully. "Occasionally challenging."

"So ..." I venture, "it's been ... working for you?"

He is open. "It's great. I love it. It's not for everybody, but I feel really blessed to have some great women in my life who share their time with me. It's wonderful." He smiles. "You should try it."

Funny man.

Michael had defied my expectations completely. If I had taken him at face value and not been paying close attention, I would have assumed that he was looking for a wife and 2.5 kids. However, by staying open to new information and keeping an open mind, I was able to more clearly understand who he was as a person.

Questioning our assumptions is the first step in discerning the true from the false. By resisting the urge to immortalize our opinions as fact, we can stay malleable to what is being revealed.

Chakras are energy centers in the body that run along the spine; each *chakra* is associated with a different element (earth, air, fire, water, ether). A modern interpretation of the *chakra* system is that each *chakra* governs different aspects of our human experience: the lower centers govern our relationship with the material world while the higher centers become increasingly etheric.

Muladhara Chakra is the "root" energy center and is situated at the base of the pelvis. The element associated with *muladhara* is earth. This chakra governs our relationships to security, stability, our bodies, and the physical world. When this chakra is deficient, we can become ungrounded, "spacey," and out of Reality. When this chakra is well balanced, we are "grounded" in the Reality of the material world.

I wound up seeing Michael a few more times. He intrigued me, and I wanted to see what it would be like to go on a date with someone who was also seeing several other women. Being a bit of a relationship adventurer, I thought that the polyamory might rub on off me.

Michael was a true gentleman, taking me out to dinner and talking about his experience of polyamory openly. However, I ultimately had to concede that it wasn't for me. Despite my occasional wildish streak, it turns that out that I am a traditionalist at heart. However, if I hadn't walked down the road a ways with Michael, I may never have confirmed that I'm a one-man only kinda gal.

FALSE PERCEPTION

Steve liked me. I mean, he *really* liked me. The night we met, he took down his Plenty of Fish profile, which is a very serious sign of intent. On our second date, he took me out for a gorgeous dinner and shared some personal news with me. Things were getting intimate!

The following weekend, he surprised me again.

> "This is from Steven." The waiter is holding a bottle of pink champagne. My roommate and I are in Whistler, celebrating her birthday.
>
> "What?" I am agog. "You are kidding me."
>
> My roommate laughs. "Who is this from?"
>
> "Oh my God, this ... this is from Steve."
>
> "Steve, Steve? Plenty of Fish Steve? The guy you've seen twice?"
>
> "Yes. He just sent us champagne. That's insane."
>
> "No, it's my birthday, he sent *me* champagne," she says tartly. "Soooo," she considers, "he's got very good sense. The way to every woman's heart is through the goodwill of

her girlfriends." She narrows her eyes at me. "So, do you like him?"

"Yeah … sure. I mean, wow, this is great."

"No, no, not just for the champagne," she flaps her hand at me. "But you know, do you *like* him?"

I pause, and nod. "I don't know him well yet, but yeah. So far, I do."

"Well." She nods at the waiter as he pops the cork. "It looks like he likes you."

Then Steve disappears.

He calls a few days later, apologizing. "Family emergency. I had to go out of town. So sorry, it's all happened so fast."

"Oh, no, how terrible!" I'm dismayed by the news. "My goodness, of course, do what you need to do!"

Two weeks go by, though, and there is still no sign of him. I send him a few encouraging texts. They go unanswered. Boy, I think, things with his family must be really tough.

After three weeks and no news, I start browsing around Plenty of Fish again. And wouldn't you know: there's Steve, with a new profile up, under a new name.

Ruh-roh.

"Oh my God," I say.

"What, what?" My roommate hurries over.

"Look!" I point at the screen.

She peers at it. "That's what's his name."

"Yes, it's Steve."

"Steve ... Champagne Steve?"

"Yes."

"Huh. I thought he was out of town?"

"I did too!" I pause. "There must be an explanation."

"Yeah, like, he wants to meet other women."

"Oh c'mon," I stammer, "you don't think the profile could mean something else ... like, he's putting it up for a friend, or ..." I trail off.

"No."

"Or maybe he's just—"

"No."

"Huh." I say, getting angry. "I don't get it. I thought he really liked me. That is weird."

She shrugs. "Maybe he did like you. Apparently not enough. But," she says, squeezing my shoulder with affection, "you had excellent timing. We did get some very nice champagne."

False Perception occurs when we experience the outside world and interpret it in a way that doesn't align with how things really are.

Vrttis – Viparyaya

One kind of thought pattern that we experience is "False Perception" (***viparyaya   vrtti***) or "misconception." False Perception occurs when we misperceive Reality. Understanding that we are making assumptions is the first step in disentangling our own agendas from our experiences. Are we perceiving Reality as it is, or are we distorting our experience based on our own desires?

Similar to my experience with Ethan, I had been creating a version of Reality that wasn't true. In my Steve experience, attentive Steve + making an effort with the champagne = he really likes me! So what the heck happened? I wanted there to be an explanation for his behavior that didn't involve me being so dead wrong. But it was hard to fight with the Reality of the profile of "MrBlueEyes1971."

Why was I so resistant to the truth that he had moved on?

Because I had liked him.

Or more accurately, I'd liked the idea of him.

I did not want the obvious version of events to be true. I wanted the implausible, magical, unicorn version of Reality where he still liked me and something crazy had somehow gotten in the way of our inevitable nuptials. His account had been hacked! Someone was masquerading as him! He'd reposted his account to do a favor for a friend!

I didn't want to give up my happy story where I had a suitor and an exciting, blossoming romance. Steve—for a few weeks at least—had covered up my Missing Piece.

But in order to be in Reality, I was going to have to recognize that I had been misperceiving the signs. Steve had ghosted on me. It was time to put on my big girl pants and accept the truth.

I wanted some closure on the experience, so I sent him an email:

"I don't mind if you don't want to pursue a relationship, but I would have appreciated it if you had been more direct with me." To his credit, he responded, "You're right. I wish you the best."

While his answer wasn't entirely satisfying, at least I felt that I was now clearly in Reality.

Lead me from the Unreal to the Real.
Lead me from Darkness to Light.
Lead me from the Temporary to the Eternal.

—Classical yoga chant, *Brihadaranyaka Upanishad*

Here is the iconic Indian story of True and False Perception:

A man is walking back to his village at night when he sees a huge snake coiled by the side of the road. He races to the village, sounding the alarm. A snake, a snake! When the villagers bring a lamp, it turns out that the snake was really a rope. In the light of wisdom, the truth is revealed.

Here's the problem with perception in general: we can't always tell the difference between what is true and what is false. When Ethan and I went out on our date, I didn't realize that we were in different Realities. It didn't even occur to me to question my assumptions. Similarly, when Steve gave all the signs of being interested, I couldn't fathom a Reality where he was being a flake.

The villager who saw the rope *truly* mistook it for a snake.

When we recognize that everything is a hypothesis, we can increase our ability to be flexible and question our assumptions. When we go on a date, we can stay open to new information about the person that we are meeting. And when we find ourselves fighting for a particular version of events, we can dig into why we are so invested in that story being true.

Use your dating adventures to get to know your mind. Practice your true and false Reality checks. Notice when you want to gloss over or embellish stories. Instead of turning your assumptions into facts, treat the present moment as a grand hypothesis.

How can this change in perspective help you to open your mind?

PRACTICES

Journal: Expectations

- Before you meet your date, take a few moments to jot down some of your expectations.

- After your date, look back at your expectations. Which were true? Which were false? Why may you have been mistaken? What did you want?

Dating Practice: Listening

- Practice listening to what your date is saying, particularly if it's not what you want to hear (i.e., I live with my mom, I'm not interested in something serious, I hate cats, etc.)

- Don't assume you know what your date means. Question your assumptions and ask when you're unsure. Test your fact versus fiction skills.

Meditation Practice: Clarity

This is a walking meditation.

- Find a safe space to walk freely and slowly (a park, a beach, or a pedestrian walkway are nice, however you can also walk in your own home).

- Start by standing still and closing your eyes for a few breaths. Clear your expectations from your mind.

- Slowly open your eyes.

- What do you really see?

- Does anything surprise you?

- As you begin to walk, see the world as it is.

- Explore seeing the world as someone else (as an architect, as a child, as someone who loves the color green), and notice how your choice may change how you perceive what you are seeing.

Yoga Practice: Clarity

- Low lunge

- High lunge

In these lunges, test your understanding of Reality. You perceive that your hips are square; are they really? You think that your knee is over your ankle; is it?

In your physical practice, listen to everything that your body tells you. Practice non-habitual listening and allow yourself to be surprised by what you find. Rather than hearing only the loudest voices in your body (your hamstrings in a forward fold, for example), listen to the other whispers, such as your shoulders, your shins, and your back. What do you hear?

Chapter 6
VISION

"Rachel. Rachel!"

I'm at my desk.

My co-worker Larissa is laughing at me. "Where were you, honey? You were miles away."

I shake off my fuzzies. I had just had my second date with Steve—Champagne Steve. In my fantasy, Steve and I were getting married on a beach in Hawaii. And I was pregnant.

"Oh my God. I was in Hawaii."

"Well, that sounds nice. Why do you sound so freaked out?"

"I was planning my wedding."

"To who? I didn't know you were serious about someone."

"That's the thing, I'm not!" I shake my head and lower my tone to a whisper so no one else can hear. "Larissa, I was planning my wedding to this guy that I went on a date with last night. Our *second* date. I am insane."

Larissa laughs. "You, my friend, are a girl." She waves me off. "So what? You want a wedding."

"To a guy I just met?"

She raises an eyebrow. "You may not want to marry *him*, but clearly part of you wants to get married. Otherwise, why would you think about it?"

"I don't want to get married."

"Uh huh."

"I don't!"

Larissa raises an eyebrow, "Right. Because those kinds of fantasies happen when you don't want to get married. Whatever you say, my friend. Whatever you say."

I turn back to my work, baffled. I don't want to get married, do I?

I stop and hold my hand over my eyes.

Oh yes. I do.

IMAGINATION

To imagine is to be human. In fact, our ability to make stuff up is one of our special superpowers. Imagination allows us to:

- Dream

- Invent

- Create

- Plan

- Empathize

- Communicate

- Envision

Imagination is essential to healthy cognition. We need it to fill in the blanks of our knowledge so that we can operate in the world. Consider your optic nerve. Did you know that you actually have a big ol' dark spot in your vision where the optic nerve connects to the back of your eye? However, your brain smartly fills in the dark spot with what it presumes will be there and "creates" Reality for you. Your brain is constantly filling in the blanks and creating a whole story when you really only know a *part* of the story.

Yogis consider Imagination a kind of "mind stuff."

Vrtti-Vikalpa

We have already been introduced to two kinds of thought patterns: True Perception and False Perception. Imagination (***vikalpa vritti***) is the third. It is not the same as False Perception. If you recall, False Perception is mistaking a rope for a snake. Even though our mind has interpreted the sensory information incorrectly, we're still basing our thoughts on something that is in the world. Imagination is when we think that there is a snake when there's no rope there at all. We are making up Reality entirely out of our own head.

It's human nature—and one of our gifts—to create stories and imagine new possibilities. We see a bird and fantasize about the possibility of flight. We taste peanut butter and chocolate and come up with a Reese's Peanut Butter cup. We meet a guy and fantasize about a wedding.

However, our Imagination can take us down a dark path as well. When we don't recognize that Imagination isn't Reality, it can lead to:

- Projection
- Unfounded expectations
- Missing present, real-world opportunities
- Unfounded fears
- Anxiety
- Delusion
- Paranoia

Ajna Chakra

Located at our "third eye," between the eyebrows, **ajna** is the energy center for vision and imagination. When this energy center is balanced, we can use it to create a viable, exciting, and realizable vision for our future. When we don't tether this energy in Reality, we can get swept up in delusion or fantasy.

FANTASY AND FEAR

When we start dating someone, our Imagination rolls out the red carpet and starts putting on a film festival. We don't know this person, we don't know the future, and we certainly don't know what is going to happen next. The future is like the spot where the optic nerve connects at the back of the eye: blank.

Rather than sit in uncertainty, our brain creates stories to help us control our expectations and fears.

When I started fantasizing about marriage with Steve, I had no idea who he really was as a person—or if I even liked him. (And, as you know, within a few weeks I would get more information about Steve that would dismantle my wishful thinking.) However, my Imagination, eager to run away with my hopes, fabricated a delightful future scenario awash with rose-colored light.

When we start fantasizing, it's a good opportunity to take a look at what the heck is going on in our minds. These crazy daydreams are like little messenger balloons that have floated up from our subconscious to tell us our secret desires, fears, and dreams.

Because we may not be aware of these desires consciously, our Imagination may sometimes surprise us. If we're not comfortable with what they're saying about us, our fantasies may seem infantile, irrelevant, or even embarrassing.

When Larissa called me out, I immediately wanted to dismiss my marriage fantasy to Steve because I recognized its irrationality. But the truth was, part of me did want to be married again! Meeting Steve had trip-wired my own deeply held (and hidden) desire.

Owning our Imagination has two parts:

- We recognize that the fantasy is not Reality.

- We acknowledge the kernels of truth it contains.

Getting friendly with our subconscious signals is a good idea. After all, what do you think is really running the show: your superficial thoughts or your deeper subconscious?

Every fantasy that we concoct contains a golden thread of truth. If we ignore this thread, we miss the opportunity to see ourselves more clearly and to separate truth from fiction. Had I not taken the time to look at my Steve fantasy, I may have walked around with the uneasy feeling that my fantasy was *actually about Steve*, rather than about something that I wanted. I might have mistakenly thought that I was falling in love *with him*. Then I would subconsciously superimpose the veil of "You're the guy that I fantasized would be my future baby daddy husband" onto Steve every time I saw him. This superimposition would limit my ability to be in Reality and see him for who he actually was.

A **vikalpa** is a mental construct that describes the stories that we make up about an experience. Creating stories is normal. The problem comes when we decide that the stories that we've conjured are facts.

Sometimes our fantasies are joyful and positive. Like my Steve fantasy, they might reveal a great dream that we've had for a career, relationship, adventure, or family.

But sometimes our Imagination isn't quite so nice. When our "Imagination of shadows" raises its head, we instead conjure up our fears, anxieties, and worries.

If the prospect of finding someone who is a good match terrifies us, we may dwell on all the ways a relationship could end. Rather than fantasize about the good stuff, we may imagine scenarios of betrayal and abandonment. When our new person doesn't respond instantly to our text messages, we default to "He was using me!" "He got back together with his ex!" or "He has a secret wife out of state!"

> *"Worry is hoping for something bad to happen."*
> —Anonymous

Our subconscious—fearful of being hurt—can create a fantasy in which our fears play out. By peremptorily creating a worst-case scenario in our heads, we are trying to control the future and protect our hearts. While the intention of our subconscious may be self-protective in nature, left unquestioned it may thwart romance and undermine trust.

Alex and I had one of those first dates that kept getting extended because we were enjoying each other's company so much. After an afternoon of lollygagging on the beach, we started planning for dinner.

"Margaritas!" I sigh happily. "I could go for one of those."

"Ah, sounds good!" He pauses. "But I don't drink."

My Spidey senses start tingling. "Why not?"

"I'm a recovering alcoholic."

I smack my leg. "Nooooo!" I collapse back on the beach and close my eyes. Just when I like someone.

"What, what?" He laughs.

"Oh, no, Alex." I take a big breath. Then another. I am suddenly really sad. I sit up. "My dad is an alcoholic, my ex-husband, my ex-boyfriend ... I don't know."

"Is that a problem?"

I speak slowly, "Obviously, I've got a pattern here. I gotta be honest. I just don't know if that's okay with me. I don't know if I can do it. I mean, I really like you, we've had a great time, but I'm not sure if I should go down that road."

He takes a big breath and looks away. "You know, I understand."

The silence grows.

"Do you mind if I think about it?" I finally say. "I think I need to think about it."

"Of course."

Despite my anxiety about his drinking, I wanted to see Alex again. Clearly, we were attracted to each other. However, I was too scared that bad things would happen to allow the relationship to move further.

My mind kept creating and replaying scary fantasies of a future where I was embroiled in a dysfunctional relationship like my marriage (more on that in chapter twelve). I caught myself thinking up worst-case scenarios:

- I'd come home and find the empty liquor bottle under the sink,

- He'd say, "I don't think I really have a problem," before cracking open a beer,

- It'd be ten years into the future, and I'd be a single mom while he was in rehab.

I was making up a lot of scenarios in my head as a way of protecting myself from an uncertain future. I was so scared that I would re-create my relationship with my ex-husband that I couldn't see Alex for who he was.

If I wanted to give this relationship a shot, then I had to own my fears.

"If you ever started drinking again, I couldn't deal with it. I didn't leave my marriage. I stayed way too long, and it was awful." I blurt this out.

He looks at me quizzically, then nods as if it were a no-brainer. "Yeah. You should. I'd tell you that. You should go running in the other direction."

I stare at him for a moment. "Oh." I am surprised. He's not hurt. There is no "stand by your man" kind of speech, no accusations that I am being selfish or uncaring. He actually agrees with me.

I take another breath. My worst fears had been aired and I am still standing.

I nod back. "Well. Okay, then."

Once I voiced my anxieties to Alex, a weight lifted. I couldn't prevent something bad from happening, but I could be clear that I would take responsibility for my own well-being. I could listen to the warning signals, but not necessarily treat them as facts. When I started to take responsibility for my own "dark fantasy," I began to see Alex for who he was, rather than through the foggy veil of my own worry. While it would still be a while before we moved past friendship, our conversation cracked open a door of possibility for something more.

Imagination is a precious part of our human experience. As we practice recognizing its influence in our everyday thoughts and feelings, we can begin to see our assumptions and ourselves more clearly. Rather than either discarding or fully believing everything we imagine, we can cultivate compassionate curiosity about our process.

Imagination and intuition are close sisters.

Intuition is the strong gut feeling that we may have about a situation. When we experience intuition, our feeling and emotional body is piping up, even though we can't consciously identify why we feel a certain way. Intuition could be based on subconscious information. If you recall, we are only conscious of five to nine pieces of information out of 2,000,000. Intuition could be based on the 1,999,991 bits of information that lie beneath our conscious radar.

However, it's challenging for us to separate Imagination from intuition. Again, we are confronted with the limitation of our human understanding. Listening to our intuition—but also being willing to question our stories—is one of the grand dances of dating.

PRACTICES

Journal: Fantasies

For the next week, write down all your wonderful fantasies. These fantasies can be related to dating, or can be from any area in your life.

- What is the kernel of truth in each of them?

- What does the fantasy give you (comfort, hope, control)? Is there a consistent theme?

- What do your fantasies reveal about you and what you want or fear?

Dating Practice: Assumptions

Practice separating Imagination from intuition. For example, let's say that you "get a feeling" that the person you're seeing isn't totally honest. When they don't text back, the fantasy in your head may be "They're dating someone else!"

Rather than wholly dismissing or believing this thought, step back and ask yourself where this belief may be coming from. Have you been getting actual information that supports this scenario? Or is this conclusion an assumption that is based on your hopes or your fears?

Meditation Practice: Imagination

- Find your meditation seat (see chapter two for more detailed instructions if needed).

- Focus on your inhalation and exhalation.

- As thoughts come up, notice them and label them: "Thinking" or—if you notice that your thoughts are clearly fabrication—label them "Imagination."

- Be curious.

- Observe how much your mind fabricates and about what.

- After your meditation, reflect: where did your mind tend to go?

Yoga Practice: Vision

- Warrior II

- Side angle pose

Do a virtual yoga practice.

Rather than do the poses physically, first lie in savasana (prone on your back) and imagine that you are doing the whole thing (or play the video guide and listen to it). Can you feel the practice in your body? Can you visualize yourself doing the practice beautifully? After you have imagined the practice, then do the actual poses. How was what you imagined different than what you are actually experiencing? Are there any surprises?

Before you do a challenging pose, pause and visualize yourself doing the pose with grace and ease. Did using your Imagination change your experience of the pose?

Chapter 7
HISTORY

"Oh, no, it wasn't right." I wave my girlfriend off.

"Oh, you didn't like him?"

I think about it. "No, at first I really did. I mean, Lucas is really nice. We got along really well."

Remember Lucas? I vomited all the things I liked about myself at him at Starbucks.

"Then he's not responsible, no job, lives in a basement ..."

"No, he has a good job. Loves his career, in fact."

"Then, you ... didn't find him attractive?"

"No, he's cute. In fact, at first I got all nervous around him. It's just ..."

"What?" She's exasperated.

"I don't know," I hedge. "It's just something ... Oh my God." I sit upright.

"What?" She's startled.

"He reminded me of Nathan."

"Nathan? Your cousin, Nathan?"

"Yes! That's so strange. Lucas reminds me of Nathan."

"Ah ..."

"It's eerie! He did the same lip thing that Nathan does. Oh my God, I can't believe I didn't see it until now!"

"Well, Nathan's cute."

"Yeah," I wave her off. "Nathan's totally cute! But I can't date my cousin." I look at her in consternation. "C'mon. Ew."

MEMORY

So far, we've looked at a few different types of thought patterns: True Perception, False Perception, and Imagination. However, there is one more powerful mind hamster at work, and it colors all of our experiences:

Smrti is "memory," the fourth kind of vrtti. *Smrti* is at work when we think about a previous experience.

Memory operates on both a conscious and subconscious level. When we use our Memory consciously, we delve into the rich storehouse of our past to gain information that is relevant to the present moment. For example, we might use Memory to answer questions such as "When is Marni's birthday?" "Where did I leave my keys?" or "Have I met this guy before?"

Most of the time, however, Memory operates subconsciously to orient us in the present moment.

Imagine that you are a passenger in a new car.

The car is your physical body, your soul is the passenger, and the highway is the journey of your life. When you are born, your car is immaculate. Ah, what a new car smell! Even the little space deep in the bottom of the cup holder is clean. The windows of your car are spotless, and everything that you can see out the windshield is clear and undistorted.

Then you start driving. You go everywhere. You drive through the dust of the desert, the pollen of the spring flowers. Soon your new car isn't so pretty anymore. Life has happened.

At first, your windshield wipers do a good job of clearing the junk off your windshield. Sure, there are a few dirty streaks, but you can still see outside. Then you have the great idea of going off-road on an adventure. Soon your car is covered with mud and bugs.

Everything that you now perceive through the windshield is seen through a thickening layer of grime from the road already traveled. In fact, pretty soon, you can't see anything out of the window without first seeing what's already on the glass. Over time, you may even forget that there was a clear sightline to begin with because now your world is seen entirely through the distortion of your smudgy, bug-covered windshield.

You see the present through the lens of the past.

Setting aside the idea of past lives for a moment, we can probably agree that we are born with a relatively clean slate of perception. However, as we begin to experience life—whether that experience is good, bad, sad, safe, scary, loving, or unhappy—we start relating everything that is happening in the present moment to our previous experiences. Our clever mind starts to create generalizations, infer meaning, and manufacture patterns.

For example, on a very practical level, when I see a chair, I know it is a chair because I have learned that there exists some sort of "chairiness" in the world. Chairs have a seat, four legs, and are designed for humans to sit upon. In the world of relationships, I know that I have met a good man or woman because he or she acts in ways that I have previously perceived as "good."

While Memory provides us with the wisdom of experience, it also makes it impossible for us to have a truly fresh experience. Your ego (sense of self) and your Memory are constantly in cahoots to navigate your situation.

During my first meeting with Lucas, the conversation in my head went something like this:

Senses (eyes): There is a guy sitting across from me. He is curling his lip.

Ego (sense of self): Hey, Memory, who does he remind me of?

Memory (consulting your previous experiences): He's acting like our cousin Nathan! He's doing that thing that Nathan does with his lip.

Ego: Yes, the thing with the lip! Ohhhh, that's cute.

Memory: Cousin Nathan is nice. He gave us his Skittles when we went to the movie with Aunt Anita. We like him.

Ego (with some exasperation): Yes, we feel good about him. But now we are definitely not attracted to him. Dating our cousin? Ew.

It's important for human efficiency that this process is largely subconscious; just think about everything you would have to remember consciously in order to drive a car! However, the subconscious nature of this process means that you will run on autopilot unless you check your assumptions. My mind couldn't help but perceive that my date looked like my cousin Nathan. However, once I recognized my association, I could detangle the past from the present and choose whether or not to give this guy a second chance on his own merit. If I hadn't taken the time to question where my association was coming from, I would just have thought, "Ew, incest," and left it at that.

Voila! Here is another moment where our yoga practice can help us to *practice the pause* so that another voice has a chance to jump in: your higher mind.

Your higher mind has the ear of your Big Self. The higher mind is the voice that interrupts our comfortable, habitual patterns and offers a more elevated form of wisdom. It sometimes tells us things we don't want to hear, such as "you don't need another cup of coffee," "put down the ice cream," "you need to call your mom," and "stop texting that dude just because you're bored." Listening to my higher mind may mean that I stop making my "I'm-going-to-eat-my-feelings-now-popcorn" and instead sit on my mat and take ten deep breaths.

While the higher mind is usually offering sage counsel, following its advice requires attention, time, and energy.

Buddhi is the voice of our higher mind and expresses our capacity to think and act beyond the instinctive level of ego and memory. *Buddhi* is connected to intuition and wisdom.

In my dating scenario, my higher mind may have chosen to interject and question my assumptions.

Higher Mind: Hey, uh, guys, so this guy reminds us of Nathan?

Memory: Yes, that thing with the lip, that's totally Nathan.

Higher Mind: But ... we know that he's not Nathan, right? This guy ... he's a totally different guy.

Ego: No, he's really like cousin Nathan.

Higher Mind: Um, no, he has a mannerism like Nathan. He's not Nathan.

Ego: Huh. I don't know how I feel then. I don't like not knowing how to feel.

Higher Mind: I know it's uncomfortable. But it's more honest. We may like him; we may not. The lip thing is not really a good metric, dig? We need more information.

Ego (grudgingly): Okay.

As we've discussed, dating takes us into the treacherous waters of uncertainty. When faced with the unknown, the mind will scramble to relate your situation to a previous experience so that you can avoid getting hurt. Do you like him or her? Do you dislike him or her? Does he or she remind you of someone?

How often do we allow a previously held experience dictate the potential of the current moment? While our associations are sometimes obvious ("He reminds me of my ex," "He seems like a nice guy," "He looks like a serial killer"), they are also rampant in our day-to-day life ("I'm a bad cook," "I'm not good at math," "I can't do a handstand").

Derailing our assumptions can help us open to possibility.

Once we recognize that memory is a natural part of how our minds navigate the world, then we can be on the alert for when our perception of the past is limiting our present possibilities.

"Be on the alert for when your perception of the past is limiting your present possibilities."

THE EXPECTATION TRAP

Expectations—born from our memories—are like comfy snuggle blankies. How wonderful when life turns out the way we expect. Yay! Success!

While having expectations is normal, they can become traps when we become attached to them. Left unquestioned, expectations become self-limiting beliefs.

> "Zach uses expressions like, 'It's a goodly brick of cheese,'" I say to my roommate. "Why not just say, 'It's a lot of cheese'?"

> "So?"

> "So ... it's not very manly, is it? 'Goodly brick,' I mean, that's just not what a guy says. He also says, 'tummy troubles.' He sounds like he's from the 18th century."

My roommate looks at me quizzically. "Where are you getting these ideas?"

"I dunno ... it's just, my dad would never say something like that. My dad wouldn't say that he had "tummy troubles.""

"... Your dad is an ex-Marine."

"So?" I say defensively.

"So ..." my roommate searches for the right words. "Zach's description of cheese is just a description. It doesn't mean he's not a manly kind of man or isn't strong." She turns to me. "Look, your version of 'guy-ness' is based on your dad, who runs a ranch with gigantic farm equipment because he finds it relaxing. Men like your dad aren't the only kind of men out there."

"Huh." I frown. "I need to think about that."

"Think about it. And while you're thinking, hand me that stalwart cube of butter."

Memories of our role models naturally define our expectations for relationships. However, if I continued to believe that someone had to own farm equipment to be a "real" man, I would have to move to Texas. And I would not have had the opportunity to discover that Zach—despite his Victorian verbiage—was strong, resilient, and masculine in his own way.

To create a conscious relationship, we must question our expectations and assumptions. While my farm equipment assumption is fairly innocent, we may have other expectations about relationships that are less benign. It's important to examine our relationship role models and histories in order to assess if our beliefs serve our future vision for partnership.

Sauca is "purity" and is an important yogic guideline that invites us to get clear and clean with our lives. This clarity includes wiping the filters of our perception clean so that we see the world as it is.

For example, I have an expectation that relationships require deep self-sacrifice. Because of this belief, I have failed to share my needs with my partner, which is clearly unhealthy (more on "sacrifice" in chapter twelve). Now that I am aware of this expectation, I can do the work to craft a relationship that values mutual support.

Understanding that our mind is limited by previous experience is the first step to expanding our sense of possibility. If we don't realize that our perception of the world is based on our previous events, then we're stuck in the dirty car and don't know it. But once we remember that we are inside the car, we can remember that there is a big, wide world of possibility outside.

SAMSKARA

Deeper patterns that drive our behavior are called *samskaras*. From a neurological perspective, we might think of these as the patterns that are created when neurons continue to fire and wire together over a long period of time.

Samskara

> "The scars of **karma**," **samskaras** are deep and well-worn grooves of conditioning that determine our thoughts, behaviors, likes, and dislikes. From a yogic perspective, *samskaras* are formed by the accumulated actions (*karma*) of many lifetimes. Shifting these deeply unconscious patterns requires patience and compassion.

Addressing our deep habits takes mindfulness and compassion. I'm also a fan of therapy. If you recognize that you are repeating the same pattern over and over (running away, rushing in, emotionally withholding, self-sacrifice), take a step back and *practice the pause*. With patience and care, we can begin to change these deeply carved grooves. By mindfully catching ourselves in the small daily moments, we can lovingly redirect ourselves toward different futures.

"Two paths diverged in the wood, and I took the one less travelled by, and that has made all the difference."
—Robert Frost

While it may be easier to follow a well-worn hiking route, you can blaze a new path for yourself if you're willing to get a little sweaty. Your past informs—but does not determine—your future.

LOVING OUR LIMITATIONS

Our relationships provide an intimate testing ground to question our stories. We begin to see the mind hamsters at work and can start to discern when they are spinning Truth, Fiction, Imagination, or Memory.

"You're over-thinking again," says Zach.

"I am not," I snap.

"Right," he looks at me pointedly. "That's not you over-thinking."

"I wasn't over-thinking," I say tartly. "No," I clarify, "I was remembering."

"Yes, and what precisely are you remembering?"

"I was remembering that the last time you asked me if I wanted to go away for a weekend, you got mad when I said that I was busy."

"I was disappointed. I wasn't mad," Zach says.

"You didn't talk to me for two days."

"I believe that you are exaggerating."

"You didn't talk to me for two days," I repeat emphatically.

"I believe," he returns with equal emphasis, "that I was busy. I was on a very busy job. I wasn't mad."

"Well, you seemed mad. I thought you were avoiding me."

"Avoiding you?" He laughs. "That's absurd. I mean," he amends, seeing my look, "I can see why you may have thought that, but that simply wasn't what was going on. I was probably just disappointed. This was," he declares grandly, "a misinterpretation. You put two and two together and came up with five."

"… Right."

He looks at me. "So … is that what you were remember ing?"

"Yes."

"Ah, okay. So …" He pauses. "Now that we've got all of that clarified … Do you want to go away with me this weekend?"

"… Can we bring a goodly brick of cheese?"

"Funny girl."

Can you see here how both False Perception and memory are at work? Throw in a dash of Imagination, and it's a recipe for misunderstanding!

Now, let's be clear: there's nothing wrong with the nature of our minds. **However, our work is to stay present and not *automatically believe everything we think.***

We are embodied in a human suit, and our souls' experiences are limited and shaped by our human perceptions. While these limitations require some questioning, they are also a source of our unique beauty. There is no other you: no other human has your mind, your body, your memories, your thoughts, or your interpretations. While your experience may limit how you see the world, it is also what makes you completely unique.

When you honor both the beauty and the limitation of your *own* humanity, then you can begin to see how other people—including your partner—are experiencing the world through their own unique lens of experience and expectation. From this perspective, we can cultivate compassion for someone else's experience, even when it's radically different from our own. Each person that you encounter is a unique expression of a soul in a human form. And each of us is flawed, limited, beautiful, and magnificent.

Our capacity to question our habitual assumptions allows us to become more intimate and connected with others. Rather than remain stuck in our version of events, we start to crack open our expectations. We become more flexible and curious. From this space of openness, we can experience others more fully and authentically for who they are. When we undertake this investigation, we are setting the foundation for intimacy and love.

PRACTICES

Journal: Excavation

- Reflect on a key moment in your dating life or relationship. What did this moment teach you? How do you experience this lesson echoing into the present moment?

- Is there a consistency to the kind of person that you have been attracted to? Is there any downside to this habitual attraction that is worth questioning?

Life Practice: Staying Flexible

- Challenge a small daily habit. Change your morning beverage, take a different route home, or go somewhere new for lunch.

- How does the small change make you feel? How might this relate to other changes in your life?

Dating Practice: Memory

Start noticing the impact of Memory in your interactions. When you are speaking to someone, how often do you go to the past to understand something?

Who does your date remind you of, and how does that shape your perception of your interaction?

Meditation Practice: Association

- Find your meditation seat (see chapter two for more detailed instructions if needed).

- Take a few deep breaths.

- Rather than avoid thinking, instead, allow your stream of consciousness to arise.

- As you catch yourself thinking, notice with curiosity how your mind has spun from thought to thought, based on associations that you've created.

- Stay with the "watching thought stream" process for several minutes.

- When you have finished your meditation, reflect on what you experienced. Can you see that your mind is actually doing this all the time and directing your experience, you just generally aren't aware of it?

Yoga Practice: Transformation

- Chair

- Twisted chair

- Twisted lunge

Notice when you compare your practice to the past. Can you be freshly in this moment without reference to a previous experience? Can you clear the windshield of your expectations in order to be in the present moment?

Chapter 8
INTEGRITY

He did all the right things.

On our first date, Brant took me out to see flamenco dancing. He held open the doors, asked me about myself, and insisted on paying the check. And yet, at the end of the night, I didn't feel the spark.

> "This has been really fun," he says. "I'd love to see you again."
>
> My stomach clenches up. I want to run away. I hate this moment.
>
> I could smile brightly and say, "Me, too!" and then avoid his texts by feigning illness or extradition. But I can't get around the fact that deliberately withholding the truth in these moments feels like a lie.
>
> When we hear the clear voice of "not the one," how do we extricate ourselves with integrity? What does compassion look like when it comes to saying "no?"

Nice Versus Good

I spent a few decades being confused about the difference between "nice" and "good."

When I was living in New York City, I played the Nurse in a rock opera production of *Romeo and Juliet* at La Mama Theatre in the East Village. (Imagine rapping, "He's dead, he's dead, he's dead, he's dead. Alas the day, he's gone, he's killed, he's dead.") A stocky, wisecracking Greek guy from Queens played the role of the villain Tybalt. Well, Tybalt asked me out on a date. Although he was an attractive guy, I didn't feel a spark.

I demurred. "Thanks, but, well, I'm not dating right now."

Then I promptly turned around and dated Mercutio and tried to keep it on the down low. Tybalt, not quite as demur, found out (because, duh, news travels fast when you're in all in the same production) and called me.

"Hey, you're dating Mercutio."

I flush in mortification. "Ohhhhhhh ..."

"Why did you say you're weren't dating?"

"Ummmmm ... I don't know, I felt ... I thought ... I didn't want to ..."

"Look," he huffs impatiently, "it's fine to not be interested, but just don't *lie* about it."

Tybalt, you may have missed your mark in killing Romeo, but your comment to me was right on target.

I was desperate to be liked. When Tybalt asked me out, I believed that if I had been forthright and honest about my feelings, he wouldn't like me anymore. He would be disappointed. He would be hurt. He wouldn't find me attractive. He might even get mad at me.

Ironically, by being "nice," I had generated precisely the result that I had most feared.

Like most of us, I got the following messages as a kid:

"Play nice."

"Don't hurt people's feelings!"

"If you can't say something nice, don't say anything at all."

And then there's this one: "Don't tell a lie."

What do we do when these messages conflict?

It's hard for our parents to explain the difference to our five-year-old selves. "Rachel, when Allie takes your My Little Pony, and you feel angry and scream that you hate her, is there a better way to communicate your feelings honestly that doesn't condemn her personhood?"

When we're kids, we aren't wired for emotional sophistication. So our parents give us the cliff notes: "play nice." When "nice" and "honest" square off, we are confused about what to do. We bring this confusion forward into our adult lives and continue to play out our playground dynamics in our intimate relationships.

As adults, we have the opportunity to consciously clarify and upgrade these old confusions. We can choose to widen our understanding of compassion beyond a childlike understanding of "nice."

Despite what we may tell ourselves, lying is rarely compassionate. It's usually about control.

We spend a lot of time jockeying for control, attempting to make the world—and the people in it—behave in a way that makes us feel safe and secure. Being honest can feel scary if we are afraid of how someone is going to react to our candor. When we're delivering unpleasant news, honesty may mean opening ourselves up to a negative reaction.

If I had told Tybalt directly that I wasn't interested in him, it is quite possible that he would not have "liked" me anymore.

But which course of action would have been more respectful? To deprive him of a candid response because it made my world more comfortable, or to share information that would empower him to protect his emotional well-being?

Compassion means acting with empathy for someone else's suffering and experience. When we remain silent or distort the truth, we are depriving someone else of important information that would enable him or her to make his or her own best decision. While it may seem superficially kind to lie to someone, in reality, we are reducing his or her potency for our own convenience.

When it comes to romantic relationships, open and clear communication is intrinsic to a healthy dynamic. Withholding information from our partners isn't nice; it undermines the trust that is the bedrock for healthy intimacy. Relationships happen in the space between two people. Clear communication keeps the water of interchange clean, fresh, and healthy. Deception—no matter how well intended—fosters weeds, scum, and sickness.

When we distort the truth, not only is it confusing for the other person, it also compromises our own integrity.

After I lied to Tybalt, I had to edit myself continually around him. I could not be my authentic self. That was, until he discovered the truth. And then, much to my chagrin, he saw me for who I really was.

Honesty liberates us from confusion. Honesty is living with our eyes wide-open, with our hearts and minds clear. Honesty clears away the drama of deceit, the self-consciousness of doubt. Honesty is the clean lines of the desert landscape. The naked rocks of the ocean. The tremendous beauty of the vast night sky.

It's your truth.

Honesty isn't always "nice." But it is ultimately *good.*

HONESTY

If you recall from chapter four, the first guideline for worldly interaction is *ahimsa*, which is nonviolence, or compassion.

The second guideline is *satya*, or truthfulness.

Satya

The second great guideline for conduct, truthfulness keeps our mind calm and unfettered. When we lie, our minds are frequently anxious and divided. Truthfulness helps us to remain steady and clear. Not only does this **yama** invite us to be truthful with others, but it also reminds us to be truthful with ourselves.

Here's the tricky part: embracing truthfulness isn't as simple as blurting out everything that we're feeling and thinking. As the yamas suggest, honesty rests in the wider arms of nonviolence and compassion. Without compassion, blunt honesty can be needlessly hurtful and self-serving.

As a teacher trainer, I often go to classes that are taught by other teachers. When I feel the compulsion to give the teacher honest feedback "for their own good," I have to do an internal check to see if this "honesty" is coming from a place of compassion ("I want you to be the best teacher that you can be"), or ego ("I need to feel important and smart"). Truth that arises from compassion—rather than ego—is the truth worth sharing. As mindful yogis, our practice is to discern when honesty will serve the highest good.

At the end of my date with Brant, I didn't need to disclose a laundry list of reasons why I thought the relationship wouldn't work. Outlining our perceived incompatibilities could have been needlessly hurtful. However, I did need to make sure that I communicated my intentions clearly so that he wasn't confused by my ambiguity.

"You know, this is a good time for a check in," I say to Brant slowly.

I try to *practice the pause.* I know from experience that I have to slow down when I talk about something uncomfortable. The first couple of times I tried to be honest at the end of a date, I pretty much vomited, "It's-been-nice-but-I-don't-think-we're-a-match-thank-you-so-much-goodbye" and then ran away.

So now I take a breath. Recovering niceaholic. Baby steps. If I'm going to say something that's hard to hear, then the least I can do is be present for it.

"This was a really great date," I continue. Something in my tone alerts him.

"Uh-oh," he says. "Ruh-roh Shaggy."

I have to laugh. "I had a really nice time," I say sincerely. "You were obviously very thoughtful and chose a really fun night for us. But for me, I don't feel like we're quite the right match. But I really appreciate your time tonight and your consideration."

"Awwww, I thought it was going well."

"It was fun," I say.

"Well," he shakes it off, "thanks for being upfront about it. No seriously, I actually do appreciate it. You wouldn't believe how many times people just ghost."

How many times has your coffee date ended with "Let's talk soon," or "Sure, give me a call!" when the truth is that we know we don't feel an attraction?

Here's your practice for compassionate honesty: tell your date how you really feel at the end of your time together.

Sharing your feelings may make your date uncomfortable—it may make you uncomfortable!—but when you are honest, you are giving them valuable information so that they know how to frame their experience and where to move next. If you are not interested, then it's not enough to assume that the rejection is implicit. "Oh, well, just not calling back is the sign that I'm not interested." In the meantime, you've left someone in a state of uncertainty for several days, wondering about you and how you feel. (Remember Champagne Steve? Don't be a Champagne Steve!)

Dvesha is aversion to pain. *Dvesha* explains why we prefer to consistently resist doing stuff that is uncomfortable. However, when we put our Big Self in the driver's seat, our aversion to discomfort starts to naturally dissipate.

Being honest—even if the honest truth is that you don't know!—is liberating. Keep in mind: just because your date is not a match doesn't mean that they are not a good person. They are just not a good person *for you*. Keeping in mind that "rejection" is not personal allows you to see their good qualities (more on rejection in the next chapter).

Being honest when we may hurt someone else's feelings is hard but ultimately kind. If you're having a hard time finding a way to articulate your feelings, here are some suggestions:

- "Thank you so much for spending your time with me. At this time, I don't feel like there's the connection I need to feel in order to move forward romantically. I really appreciate your time and wish you great luck in your search."

- "Thank you for your time tonight. You know, you seem like a really kind person." Add *authentic* feedback of what you liked. "However, I feel as if we want different things/are looking in different directions."

- "Thank you for sharing your time with me. Although I really enjoyed your company and getting to know you, I'm not feeling that click that I need in order to move forward."

If you don't know what you want to do:

- "Do you mind if we have a check in? I feel like it's a good practice to be really up front after meeting someone for the first time to see where we are at...How are you feeling?"

- "I really appreciate that you took the time to meet with me. I'd love for us to be really honest with each other. I know it's scary, but we don't really have anything to lose by putting it all on the table! What are your thoughts?"

Rather than be tempted to put on the façade of "nice," it becomes our spiritual practice to find a tolerance for our own discomfort. When we are no longer afraid of being uncomfortable, then we have the option to assess the situation and decide from a higher place whether our candor or silence is the highest route to compassion.

Free up their headspace. Free up their time. Be compassionate. And be clear.

"The third enemy of compassion is idiot compassion. This is when we avoid conflict and protect our good image by being kind when we should say a definite 'no.' Compassion doesn't imply only trying to be good."
—Pema Chödrön, *The Places That Scare You*

In my experience, the reaction to this kind of truthfulness has been positive. Almost every single person, after an understandable moment of processing, has appreciated the openness and the candor and—literally—thanked me. When we are clear and respectful, we are giving them the information that they need to safeguard their affections, time, and heart.

Or course, not everyone will be quite so appreciative.

Curt invited me to an outdoor concert. He was a sweet comic book nerd (I love nerds!) and worked security in the transport industry. Because we had mutual friends that I trusted, I agreed to drive with him rather than take my own car.

Surely an outdoor concert would be fun.

> *"I want to leave," I text my roommate. "He's been talking non-stop. I can't get a word in edgewise."*
>
> *"There's a huge leak in the kitchen," she writes back.*
>
> *"What, OMG!"*
>
> *"It's everywhere. You need to come home now."*
>
> I laugh, getting it.
>
> *"Thanks, but leaving now seems selfish. Note: always self-drive."*
>
> After the concert, Curt is enthusiastic. "I knew you'd love this!"
>
> He hasn't actually asked me what I thought. I'm starting to feel like Curt is talking to his idea of me, rather than seeing who I am. I'm tired and feel a headache coming on.

"Here, take my iPad!" We get in his car, and he gives it to me. "You be DJ. Choose what you like."

I choose a song.

He shakes his head. "No, no, no, try this song," he says. "It's really good. You'll love it."

I had liked the song that I'd chosen, but didn't push it. After a long ride back to the city, we arrive at my car. Gentlemanly, he jumps out to walk me to the door.

He's excited. "What a great concert ... what's next!"

I pause. "Well, let's talk about that for a moment." I feel uncomfortable, but I know that Curt and I are not a good match. It's better to tell him now than leave him wondering about our next adventure.

He looks at me, puzzled.

I take a breath. "Curt, you're a great guy, and I've had a nice time with you tonight, but I don't quite feel that we're syncing up in the way that I need to move forward romantically."

He shakes his head, confused. "What do you mean?"

"I don't think our interests are the same."

"Sure they are."

"Curt, I'm like opera ... you're like ..."

"Rock and roll?"

I smile, relieved. "Yeah."

He puts up his hands, looks down, and starts backing to his car. "Don't give up on me just yet."

I'm confused. I shake my head and try to call after him, "It's not about giving up on you. You're not doing anything wrong. You're great. I just don't think we're right for each other."

He hedges, "Ah, I don't know. Just, just don't give up on me yet." He gets into his car and drives away.

Not matching up with someone isn't a comment on his or her personhood. There's a gal out there who is perfect for Curt. It's just not me. I shake my head.

Well, at least I told him. Telling him now is better than walking around with the queasy, unfinished feeling that I would have if I had remained silent.

The next day, I get a text:

Rachel, thanks for coming out. I had a great evening at the concert. Right up until the point where you kicked me in the balls.

Ah. Well.

Balancing *ahimsa* and *satya* isn't always easy, or always clear. In your search for a partner, you will probably connect—and disconnect—with many people. Not every encounter will end on a happy note.

There are, unfortunately, a terrible amount of publicized examples online (like Instagram's Bye Felipe) that detail cruel, immature, and even shocking responses to an honest exchange.

Although in my direct experience it's been rare, people use these communication channels to lash out.

- "Your loss."

- "Ungrateful slut."

- "Frigid bitch."

An important caveat to online (or in person) communication: there is absolutely no need to respond to communication that is frightening, aggressive, distasteful, or overtly sexual. Many women and some men have reported feeling threatened or harassed—especially in online dialogues.

When someone is malicious, it's best to follow the advice of another yoga sutra to "disregard the wicked" (sutra 1.33). Do not hesitate to block and report users whose communication is off-color. Upholding others is not just about compassion but may also be about creating strong boundaries (more on this in chapter twelve).

Sometimes your attempts at honest and compassionate communication may fall on defensive ears. However, do you really want to date someone who has a hard time hearing about your honest experience? Their inability to hear your truth doesn't bode well for conversations that are of real importance, such as where you should send the kids for school, or how to address your mom's need for a nursing home.

Remember Alex? We hit a road bump early on in our relationship. I met him at a Starbucks to have "the conversation." Because we'd seen each other more than a few times, it was important to me to meet him in person.

Alex walks in, sees my face, and doesn't bother to order anything.

We look at each other.

"Look," I start. As always, I get squirmy. My chest feels tight. "I just don't think that this is working. There are too many things that—"

He interrupts, rather gently, "Hey, it's okay. I think I behaved like a jerk. We don't have to go through a list of reasons why this won't work unless you want to?" He means this sincerely.

"No," I say, surprised. "I don't need to."

He pauses. "Okay. Honestly, you're the first person I've connected with in a long time that I've really liked. It's been great to feel that again, and I'm grateful that I met you. And I wish you nothing but the best."

I nod.

He stands up. "Hug?"

I give him a big hug.

He steps back. "I suppose we could say that we'd stay in touch, but ... we probably wouldn't." He smiles. "Take care."

"Uh, you, too," I say. I watch him leave, feeling oddly bereft. I'm impressed by his honesty and openness.

I sit back down and think.

Road bumps always happen; it's how we deal with them that is important. Alex's accountability and grace were so impressive that I realized he was someone worth knowing better. We stayed in touch, and eventually, our friendship turned into something more.

INTEGRITY

When we align ourselves with the wisdom of our Big Self, we are cultivating and strengthening an inner sense of worthiness and solidity that is separate from the outside world. This is integrity.

"We act with integrity because we want to uphold our values; not because of the affirmative response that we will get from the outside world."

When someone is defensive or angry because they don't want to hear about your feelings, your practice is to uphold the integrity of your action and character without external validation.

Their response—positive or negative—is less important than upholding your values.

During dating, taking these small steps to practice self-validation helps prepare you for the spiritual work of communicating difficult truths when the stakes are higher. In the wider view, your truth creates trust, which is more important than a momentary emotional feeling of being uncomfortable.

After I started my online dating quest, someone began creating fake and salacious profiles of me and then began communicating with other men as my avatar. I first heard about the profiles through someone I'd dated.

"Nice sexy new profile, Rach!" I get the text from David. We'd gone on a few dates, and then we'd had an honest conversation that it wasn't going to go further. He is a dynamic and interesting man, and we had left things on a positive and friendly note.

"What do you mean," I text back.

"... That's not you?"

"What's not me?"

I check out the profile, called "SexyRachel." There are photos of me that have been hacked from other online sites and from (alarmingly) my private email correspondence. The profile is sleazy, demeaning, and sexualized.

- "My nickname is Stiffy Nips, and I might respond really well if you call me that."

- "I have dated wealthy men and been a piece of ass on the side."

- "After my divorce, I became attached to my Hitachi Magic Wand (a vibrator). I'd even give it a grateful kiss at night."

- "Come to my yoga class and watch me! But don't tell me. I like it when I'm not sure if you're there ..."

I felt shocked, shaken, and humiliated.

I reported the profile to OkCupid and to the police. After it was taken down, another profile popped up in its place. Again and again. The profiles became increasingly demeaning. Men began contacting me through my website and Facebook page to continue the "conversation."

"Sorry, not me," I'd write back. "You've been had. You've likely been corresponding with some middle-aged dude in a basement."

Though I filed several police reports, they couldn't do anything legally without a physical threat. I had a choice: pursue a civil suit, or let it go.

I took a breath, stepped back, and considered my options. My Big Self was watching as my Little Self had a storm of feelings and outrage. What was truly of value to me here? What was the highest course of action?

If I chose to panic over these profiles—and invest in a civil court case—I would be spending a lot of time and energy to find "justice" and defend my image. Was that really how I wanted to spend my time and energy? Was I going to define my sense of self by what others might think, or by what I thought?

Here—albeit in a strange package—was another opportunity to practice self-reliance and self-trust. Another opportunity to remember that internal worthiness cannot be found in an external source.

Choosing to rely on our own internal sense of goodness helps us to put our Big Self in the driver's seat. By choosing to act with purpose and integrity, we are upholding our higher values regardless of personal inconvenience and discomfort.

And—on all levels—isn't that what humanity needs?

Practices

Journal: Nice Versus Good

- What looks like "nice" to you?

- Do you equate compassion with softness or passivity? What might vigorous, active compassion look like?

- Think of an example from your life when you valued truth over "niceness." Now think of an example where you chose niceness over truth. How did you feel in each case?

Dating Practice: Honesty

- First Date Practice: at the end of a first date, initiate a proactive, upfront conversation with your date about how you both feel and if you want to move forward (even if the answer is "I don't know").

  o Practice courageous authenticity and admit your own true feelings to yourself.

  o Ask yourself: am I choosing this course of communication for my own comfort levels, or for the greater good of the person in front of me and myself?

- If you've met someone in person more than once, ending the exchange via text is no longer appropriate. If you need to have an honest conversation, do it over the phone or in person.

- Use language that requires you to own your truth, rather than making it about them. For example, "I feel this way …" rather than "You make me feel …"

Meditation Practice: Compassion and Truth

- Stand or sit in front of a mirror.

- Meet your own eyes.

- Can you see yourself truly? Are there parts of yourself that you would prefer to avoid?

- Bring to mind someone who you love and imagine them seeing you.

- See yourself with eyes of both truth and love.

- Practice courageous and radical self-acceptance.

Yoga Practice: Fortitude

- Chair

- Dolphin plank

This week, practice cultivating fortitude in your yoga practice. We often want to check out of a yoga pose as soon as it becomes uncomfortable. Can you stay in the discomfort of the practice in order to become stronger? Can you sacrifice your own temporary convenience for a greater ideal?

Chapter 9
REJECTION

In the last chapter, we looked at the spiritual opportunity of being forthright with someone else about our feelings when we want to say no. But what do we do when someone rejects us?

Call. Call. Call. Call.

I'm staring at my phone, willing it to ring.

I'm trying not to stare at my phone.

I sigh.

I lower my standards: Text. Text. Text. Text.

I will my phone to buzz.

Maybe it's off.

I check it.

It's on.

Maybe it's on "do not disturb."

I check it.

It's not.

Nothing.

But the silence is speaking volumes.

In the past, I was relentless in my affections. I thought that if the guys I liked just *knew me* well enough, surely they'd realize that I was completely wonderful, and they would fall in love with me immediately. Convinced that these men were shy, intimidated, or simply very badly confused, I'd throw myself into their lives like a lounge singer sprawling across a fat baby grand.

The first boy that I ever loved looked like the love child of C. Thomas Howell and Robert Sean Leonard. His name was Geoff. I was fifteen. In the face of his disinterest, I was steely-eyed, irrepressible, and resolute.

"I will make him mine. I don't care if he is dating Laura, the blond and sporty senior, I will become his confidante and soul mate. I will become his very best friend, and he will reveal all his secrets only to me."

This is literally—*literally*—what I thought.

Through sheer honey badger tenacity, I managed to wedge myself into Geoff's life like Play-Doh squished into a pasta mold. It wasn't pretty, but it worked. Once I felt appropriately lodged, I let out a big sigh of relief. *Ahhhhhh!* I thought, *we may not be dating per se, but we are friends. I am in the inner sanctum!* Wipe brow. Mission accomplished.

I'd love to chuckle ruefully and pass off my neediness as youthful folly. But fast-forward twenty years, and I'm doing exactly the same thing.

When my marriage ended (more on that saga in chapter twelve), I was devastated. Until my divorce, I hadn't understood how "heartache" could be literal. There was a huge, gaping hole in my chest.

Not only was I freshly separated from my husband, but I had also just moved to a new country, changed coasts, shifted careers, and taken over the mortgage on our apartment. My family was a country away. I had no friends, no support network, and I worked a lonely stay-at-home job as a commissioned sales agent for a software company. Discovering late-night parties with a sweet and sympathetic group of ravers felt like instant connection, generous love, and healing acceptance.

The ecstasy may have helped just a teensy, tiny, little bit.

I dated one of the leaders of this partying crowd on and off for a couple of months. You met Jeremy in chapter two; he's the filmmaker who was conveniently out of town for weeks at a time. Smart, confident, and understated, he had a cute habit of adjusting his glasses by holding the frames with his thumb and middle finger and sliding them up his nose. He also had a cute habit of being attracted to really fucked up women.

In short, he was perfect for me.

Jeremy was charismatic, smart, distracting, and too far away—both physically and emotionally—to see how messed up I really was. At least at first.

Then he came back into town from work. The sweet allure of my "damsel in distress" status soured in the face of how desperately I needed his attention.

He calls while I'm driving.

"Yeah ..." he sighs. "Look, this isn't working for me."

I am on my way to my lawyer's office to sign the papers that will finalize my legal separation from my husband. My chest tightens. I pull my car over. My breath gets fast. My world slides.

"Not working for you."

"Yeah ... sorry. You're just ... it's too much. You're too ..."

"What?"

"Well ... you're ..." He sighs. "Needy."

I feel as if a hot stone has been set on my chest. I'm stunned, then furious. "Needy." It's a vile word. "Needy."

"Needy" stabbed me straight through my feminist heart. "Needy" transformed my painful moments of vulnerability into simpering weakness. I had opened up to Jeremy at my most helpless and had then been unceremoniously kicked to the curb. Over the phone, no less.

I was furious. But underneath my anger, I was humiliated. Because he was right.

I *was* needy.

Jeremy's affection had provided a distraction from the pain of my divorce. The decline of my marriage had shattered my self-image as a confident, capable, and loving woman. In the aftermath, I felt like a failure: weak, inept, and exposed. Jeremy's attention had helped me to feel better about myself. In the light of his affection, I felt like someone who was still worthy of interest and love. And when he dumped me, the thin defense that I'd plastered over my own self-loathing blew away.

His rejection felt like death.

Literally, fear of death, ***Abhinivesa*** is our natural desire to cling to what is habitual and avoid endings and change. ***Abhinivesa*** is one of the obstacles (***kleshas***) to our practice and is said to be powerful, even in the wise.

It's human nature to be afraid of change; our minds are wired for safety and consistency. When we stand in uncertainty and change, we tenderly touch on the truth that change is inevitable.

However, even the humiliation of being dumped wasn't enough to make me step back and start taking care of myself. I couldn't bear the idea that Jeremy thought of me as weak. I craved his validation. Rather than cutting off ties with him, I wanted him to like me. I needed him to think that I was still cool.

I took on the role of the "easygoing ex" and performed a lot of tricks to make sure that he still thought that I was "okay." I was casual and distant. Flirty, but not too flirty. And sure enough, we stayed in touch and became friends. Once more, I had Jeremy's approval. Though the lamp of his affection may have dimmed, enough of it remained to restore my dignity. I was okay.

My confusion in both of these situations was simple: I had wanted Geoff and Jeremy—twenty years apart—to give me something that only I could give myself.

Self-love.

Let's not sugar coat a breakup: the end of a relationship feels like death. It is death. We are lonely and vulnerable. We feel despair, remorse, regret, anger, and self-doubt. Precisely because rejection is so painful, it exposes the very core of our Missing Piece confusion. Seen in this way, rejection becomes a potent opportunity for self-growth and fierce compassion.

THE JEWELS OF REJECTION

Rejection is full of opportunities.

Like diamonds that are created from coal under deep pressure, the "jewels of rejection" have been forged with great intensity. Out of darkness and heat, something lustrous, pure, and unbreakable is born.

The first and most important "jewel of rejection": self-love.

Call, call, call.
Text, text, text.

Rather than harden, blame, or scramble to cover our bad feelings up, we can take a breath and *practice the pause.* We can soften and remember that our Big Self is watching the show. Our Little Self is having an emotional adventure, but we are safe, whole, and worthy of love.

When we feel pained by rejection in dating, our confusion is glaringly obvious. After all, you've been on—what? One date? Three dates? Even if you've been dating someone for several months, this person's understanding of you could only begin to skim the surface of who you are. Yet you gave them the keys to self-esteem kingdom. You believe the rejection is personal.

It's often easier to believe someone else than to trust ourselves. However, running after external approval is like eating candy when you need kale: while the sugar high is a temporary fix, it is unsustainable and eventually makes us sick.

Dukha is "suffering," and is a universal human experience that occurs when we feel pain based on a misguided attachment to an external source. When we find ourselves suffering and fearful, it's a good sign that we have exported our sense of well-being to something outside of ourselves. Our pain is a signpost reminding us to come back home.

When I gave Jeremy the keys to my self-worth kingdom, I used him to cover up my inner angst and pain. When he liked me, my Missing Piece was filled. I felt so good! *The world is perfect, and I'm falling in love! I am okay!* But when he went away, the hole was unearthed again. *No! I'm humiliated, mortified, bereft.* My dependence on him was exposed.

When we feel rejected, our desire to fill our Missing Piece with the external world is revealed. We have exported our sense of worthiness into something that is temporary and external rather than remembering that our sense of wholeness must come from within. While it is natural and human for us to love others and be sad when they are gone, we can begin to recognize the difference between true loss and the desperation that arises when we have been using someone else to cover up our pain. By recognizing this difference, we can begin to become more responsible for our own sense of self-worth.

The second jewel of rejection: expanding our capacity to feel.

Understanding that we are not *defined* by our feelings doesn't mean that we should feel less. On the contrary! Feeling is the spice of life, the nectar of the peach, the icing on our cake. Feeling is a birthright of our humanity.

However, we usually don't like to feel when it feels bad. Anger? Remorse? Fear? No, thank you! We would rather stuff those feelings into our emotional closet.

But when we start editing out our bad feelings, we limit our capacity to feel the good stuff, such as joy, gratitude, and love.

When rejection conjures up challenging feelings, we can practice expanding our emotional range in a safe environment. After all, it's just dating, remember? The stakes aren't actually that high. You're safe; you're okay. While the Little Self has a wild emotional experience, the Big Self can watch with love and compassion.

By staying in our Big Self and holding space for our feelings, we can increase our capacity to feel all the colors of our emotional rainbow. No matter what happens, we stay tethered to the truth that our deepest self is good, worthy, and joyful.

"Yoga isn't about narrowing the bandwidth of our emotions but about creating a container that's vast enough to hold them with grace."

As you explore your feelings, you will discover that emotions—like thoughts—are temporary phenomena. They arise and dissipate. When we are tethered to our Big Self, we can more graciously experience a full range of emotions without shutting down, becoming reactive, or lashing out. This is good news because life brings up storms of emotions, and we want to be able to treat other people with care. Cultivating your personal equanimity will help you to navigate your feelings in any situation.

The third jewel: increasing your compassion.

Experiencing your own vulnerability also helps you to empathize more with other people. Our own pain is the window that helps us to recognize the uncertainty and angst that lies within every human heart. We are not unique in our feelings: almost every adult human has experienced love and loss. By widening our own capacity to feel, we increase our ability to relate to the experiences of others.

A final jewel: cultivating our own strengths.

Sometimes we are attracted to someone else because they possess qualities that we want for ourselves. For example, part of my attraction to Jeremy stemmed from my admiration for his success and creativity. On some level, I thought that if Jeremy liked me, then I would be validated by some sort of magical relationship transference. Jeremy was creative; Jeremy liked me; therefore, I was creative! Ta-da!

While being inspired by our partners is a good thing, substituting their success for our own means that we are missing an opportunity to follow our own hearts' longing. "Success vampirism" amplifies our Missing Piece conundrum: we can't lose the person because we are afraid that we will lose a quality that we desperately want.

"But I don't know how to change a tire." I am quiet.

Alex and I had broken up. Our relationship had lasted nearly a year. I had loved him.

A box of Kleenex has exploded in my apartment. I am curled up on the corner of my couch with one of my good friends.

"I can change a tire," Ashley speaks softly and pats my arm. "I'll show you how to do that. You can call me, and I'll help you through it."

"We were going to go camping together," I start crying. Visions of my future with Alex are dancing in my head. Exciting visions of travel, adventure—and children. "We had all these great trips planned. Exciting trips."

"You have lots of people to go camping with." Ashley cocks her head. "Marta wants to go camping. Or I'll go camping with you."

"Bu-but it's not the same."

"I know, honey. But do you really need him to do this stuff, or can you do it by yourself?"

I look at her through my watery eyes and snotty nose. Ashley doesn't mince words, and she's got that look that says she's about to smack down some wisdom.

"Maybe," she says sternly, "it's time to get out your own camping gear and go do it by yourself."

Alex had introduced me to outdoor adventure. We took trips, went hiking, and skied hard. When we broke up, I felt as if I had lost that part of myself. Without him, my inner adventure girl had disappeared.

One of the wonderful gifts of having a relationship is that it can help us discover new aspects of ourselves. Perhaps you never knew that you liked baseball, or camping, or rock climbing. Relationships can show us new landscapes within ourselves that may otherwise have remained hidden. When we break up with someone, we may be afraid that we will lose this new part of ourselves. However, you don't need to lose this new territory when the relationship ends. If you like what you discover, then continue exploring.

Sometimes a relationship can illuminate something within us that we don't love. When my ex-husband started drinking, I became a passive enabler of his dysfunction. Through this experience, I learned that I am deeply afraid of being on the receiving end of someone else's anger, and I have a hard time creating and sustaining healthy boundaries. By taking a compassionate pause and witnessing this habit, I can do my best to be alert for this pattern in the future.

Relationships are the mirrors that help us to see ourselves. Through our intimate interactions, the Reality of who we are is revealed. We may love what we discover, or we may scream in horror and want to run away. However, once we see ourselves, we can practice the pause. We can take another loving and mindful step towards being the person that we want to be.

Rejection Isn't Personal

So now, brass tacks: rejection doesn't really exist.

Rejection is a myth. Made up. Fictional.

We tend to feel rejection as a dismissal of our own personhood. However, a more accurate and Reality-based understanding would be to see that we have been *ill fitted*. Our jigsaw pieces just didn't match.

Sustainable mutual attraction requires a shared recognition of values, interests, likes, and dislikes. It's a two-way street, with both parties seeing themselves in each other. With successful partnerships, there is usually a similarity in how we view the world, what we find funny, and how we like to live. And, of course, there's probably a good ol' dose of sexual attraction.

Chances are, if your feelings are one-sided, and the other party isn't pursuing the connection, then your interest isn't based their personhood, but rather on a perceived need that he or she can fill in you. You may be imagining a connection that isn't there (there's the Imagination *vrtti*, filling in the gaps again!) in order to help justify your Missing Piece need.

When I desperately needed Jeremy to like me, I wasn't able to see him fully for himself because I first needed him to *fix my problem*. I couldn't even tell if I really liked *him* because I was too busy hiding from my own feelings to see him for who he was! It was a classic Missing Piece confusion.

Okay, but what if there seems to be an authentic mutual connection—and they still pull away?

Here's the tough part: it doesn't matter.

If they're not dancing the dance with you, then they're not the person for you. End of story. Ultimately, understanding *why* is beside the point.

When we try to rationalize and justify a rejection ("He was hung up on his ex-girlfriend," "She's not ready for a relationship," "He has a weird thing with his mother"), we are doing a tap dance to cover up the feeling that we aren't good enough. We are trying to create a story in our heads that makes us come out looking okay. Because we have forgotten that we actually *are* okay.

We don't arrive at our Starbucks date with a blank slate.

Remember the car of experience? Our windshields are full of stuff from our past that will influence how we see the world. Similarly, the person sitting across the table from you is also enmeshed in an enormous and unfathomable web of their own life experience.

Aparigraha is a yogic guideline that means "non-grasping," and it invites us to relinquish the tendency to hold on to our thoughts and cling to old ideas. Are we willing to "unstick" ourselves from our attachments to external objects (or our ideas about someone else solving our problems) in order to be free?

Your date—like you—is experiencing the world through the lens of all of their previous experiences. While we usually prefer to believe that we are the belly button of the universe, the truth is that it is not all about us. We don't have control. You cannot control—or even really understand—how they may be perceiving you. We cannot fully comprehend the complexity of the road that they have traveled.

"Let it go."
—Elsa, *Frozen*

And sometimes we just have to let go.

LEARNING TO LET GO

I fought like a banshee to stop the break-up with Alex.

When our communication started breaking down, I poured my heart out in three lengthy emails to try to bridge the gap. The night after we broke up, I showed up at his doorstep at 7 a.m. to fight for another chance.

"I know that we're having all these problems, but I love you, and I want to make this work."

I have no doubt that we both fought for the relationship as best we could. But at the end of the day (and even despite therapeutic intervention), we couldn't find our way out of our communication quagmire.

Sometimes, you have to let go.

Ishvara Pranidhana can be translated as "surrender to a higher power." As we practice letting go of our ability to control a situation, we begin to cultivate the ability to recognize what we have control over—and what we don't. "Let go and let God."

The natural world is cyclical: constantly beginning, sustaining, and dying. Seasons change, relationships change, jobs change, tides move, stars are born, stars die. Death is everywhere. Despite our mind's resistance to change, we are also part of this natural cycle. We begin, we sustain, and eventually, we dissolve.

Samhara means "dissolution" and is part of the universal cycle of generating, sustaining, and dissolving. Our suffering comes from mistaking the impermanent as permanent (*avidya*). **Samhara** is actually a reabsorption and evolution of universal energy rather than an ending or a loss. This transformative process plants the seeds for new growth and experience.

Yoga philosophy reminds us that the universe works in cycles. All material matter (*prakriti*) is continually being birthed, sustained, and then destroyed. There is also a fourth stage—the emptiness—out of which the birthing comes. This empty space is full of uncertainty and groundlessness. While we hate to rest in the terrible expanse of uncertainty, it is essential for rebirth.

Om

Om (also spelled Aum) has four parts. There is the first part, "A," which represents the beginning, or creation. The second part, "OO," represents the sustaining. The third part, "M," represents dying, or the ending. And then finally, the silence after the chant is *turiya* (the void), which contains all potentialities. And out of this void, the sound arises again.

Rejection teaches us to take a breath, let go, and trust in the new cycle that will unfold.

PRACTICES

Journal: Letting Go

Reflect upon a non-romantic situation that you have had to let go of in the past (perhaps of a job, a house, an idea).

- What did you lose?

- And what did you gain?

Reflect on endings. Do you see anything in the world that does not ultimately change or end?

Reflect upon the end of a relationship from the past.

- What was truly lost?

- What new understanding did you gain through the experience of the relationship, and how do you see the effects of that learning in your life today?

Dating Practice: Letting Go

Treat each date as an opportunity to begin, experience, and let go of expectations.

- If you knew there was no second date possible, would your experience of the date change?

- After the date is over, can you completely let go of expectations and instead rest in the space of not knowing?

Meditation Practice: Letting Go

Letting go creates space for what is next. The longer exhale in this practice encourages connecting to release.

- Find your meditation seat (see chapter two for more detailed instructions if needed).

- Focus on your breath.

- Inhale for a count of four, exhale for a count of six.

- Let each exhale be an opportunity to release.

- Each inhale is a new beginning.

- Notice the pause of possibility between the inhale and exhale.

Yoga Practice: Softening

- Sphinx

- High cobra

Find the opening and softness that is possible by breathing deeply into your heart space. Rather than hardening and forcing into your backbend, use your inhalation to create space and exhalation to soften into the space that you have created.

Chapter 10
SURRENDER

Falling in love is scary.

I meet him. I like him. Things are going okay.

But then, something changes: I start to *really* like him.

I get scared. And I start acting funny. Not ha-ha funny. Like weird funny.

Because I get worried about what he thinks.

Maybe he won't think that my references to *Star Trek* are cute, or that my tendency to belch quite loudly (got that from my dad, thanks, Dad!) isn't endearing. Maybe he thinks my funny accents are racist, or that getting weepy when I hear Shakespeare is girly and overly dramatic.

The editing begins. I stop cackling loudly or getting overly metaphysical. I don't sing out loud or wax poetic about delicious food. I start the "amplify/blandify" process. When I amplify, I trot out all the things about myself that I think will sound impressive.

> "Golly, going to Columbia was such an enlivening experience!"

> "My goodness, it was so inspiring to dissect those human bodies."

"Yes, helping the orphans was challenging, but by God, the refugees needed it."

(Okay, I didn't do that last one, but it really sounds good.)

Rather than just be who I am, I drop interesting fact breadcrumbs, as if these little nuggets will keep my date's attention and interest. Only the shiny bits, thank you very much.

When I blandify, I edit out anything potentially spicy about my personality and settle for the oatmeal.

"I disagree with you," turns into, "Wow, that's an interesting point of view."

"I feel completely anxious today," turns into, "I'm fine."

"My parents voted for Trump," turns into, "Look at that bird over there."

When we blandify, we pull in the rough edges and play it safe in the demographic center. Curtail those racy jokes! Dress only in corporate casual! And for God's sake, make excellent small talk.

When we start to *really like* someone, we usually get scared that they won't like us back. So we only share the prettiest and most acceptable parts of ourselves. While some of this is quite reasonable (come on, no one needs to see you cut your toenails at the dinner table), we often hide away the softer and more vulnerable—more human—parts of ourselves. But ironically, it is only through sharing our quirks and vulnerability that we can be authentically seen and understood. By choosing what feels like a "safe" course, not only do we undermine ourselves, but we also deprive our partners of the opportunity to see us for who we really are.

Self-Consciousness

"Don't walk like a duck!" My roommate is coaching me on how to walk in my heels.

"I don't walk like a duck," I scowl.

She rolls her eyes. "You do walk like a duck. Walk slower."

I try walking slower.

She cocks her head and squints. "Okay, now lift your knees, don't drag your feet. No, no! Not like that. That was way too much."

"You said to lift my knees!"

"I didn't say become a flamingo! Okay, okay ... that's getting better. Good, yes, you look ... almost natural."

"Look at that," I say. "I have become ... a swan."

I'm on my way to a fancy dinner.

It was only date two, but I was very excited about this new guy Steve. (Remember Champagne Steve?) In fact, I was so nervous about our second date that I went out for a pre-date run to burn off some excess steam. Date one had started off as a casual meet up that had morphed into an evening of laughter and connection. Now, for date two, he was taking me out to a dinner at a spectacular restaurant. A restaurant that required heels. I wanted to impress.

I put on an outfit and marched over to my roommate's room for review.

"Ta-da!" I strike a pose and wait for the response.

"... Are you going to someone's funeral?" she asks.

"What?" My shoulders droop. I am so not good at clothes. "I suck at this. I hate dressing up."

"Well, it's true that fashion may not be your strength," she says delicately, "but there are many things about you that are very, very loveable."

I look down at my outfit. "I look like an Italian widow."

She laughs. "Come on, let's raid my closet. I've got something fabulous you can wear."

When we start getting self-conscious, it's usually because we are afraid someone is going to find us out. The jig is up, and something terrible is about to be revealed. In my date with Steve, I was afraid that my (ahem) sporty dress style wouldn't measure up to his standards.

We all have something that we feel embarrassed about. Maybe you snore, have funky feet, or secretly eat brownies for breakfast. If you're like me, maybe you love eating gigantic bowls of popcorn like your hand is a shovel.

The self-consciousness that we feel as we start to fall in love can be a wake-up call to see if there's really anything there worth investigating. To notice, with love and care, why we're feeling embarrassed. Sometimes self-consciousness stems from a healthy desire to become better people. For example, feeling self-conscious about making an off-color joke or having a lie exposed is a good sign that we want to make some changes. Our embarrassment is highlighting the difference between who we are and who we want to be and shows us where we have some work to do.

However, sometimes we feel self-conscious about behaviors or desires that are truly harmless and indeed are part of our individual essence. We can be trained to feel bad about parts of ourselves that don't fit into a cultural standard or "norm." Physical standards of beauty are a great example. We may feel sad about our plump thighs or thinning hair because we are inundated by images of inhuman beauty standards. Or we may have a passionate hobby that others don't consider cool. Maybe your prized bug collection was ridiculed in high school, and now you're ashamed to wax poetic about your local Lampyridae.

In chapter four, we practiced revealing our authentic selves in our online profiles. Now it's time to share ourselves authentically in person and to cultivate the bravery to allow ourselves to be authentically seen by someone else. It's time to get brave and let your bug-loving, LEGO-building, popcorn-eating freak flag fly.

OPPORTUNITY: SELF-LOVE

"I love *Star Trek*." I take a deep breath and it all rushes out. "Love it, love it, love it, love it. Love everything about it. Had a major crush on Wil Wheaton. Used to read the *Star Trek* books. Long books. Four-hundred-page books. That's how much I love it."

My ears are burning.

"*Star Trek*?" Alex says, cocking his head. "What did you like about it? Like, why not *Star Wars*?"

I shake my head. "Oh no, my friend. Oh no. Not so interested in *Star Wars*. *Star Trek*, all the way. See, it's the values of the world in *Star Trek* that are so appealing."

Uh-oh, I'm starting to get earnest.

"*Star Trek* is like a utopian version of who we can be. Humanity, that is. I mean, we have all these dystopian versions of reality in our culture, post-apocalyptic stuff. Visions of people being their worst. You know, like *Terminator* or *Aliens*. But *Star Trek* is a positive version of what we can become. You know, using technology wisely, grappling with our humanity, valuing education and exploration."

"So you love *Star Trek* for its values?"

"Yes," I say, self-consciously and with just a wee bit of defiance. "I do."

"Hmmmm." Alex seems to be taking this all in. "So I guess there's really just one question that I have."

"What?"

He looks at me sideways. "Picard or Kirk? Or are you a Janeway kinda gal? Or I suppose we could throw Pike in there, too, if you want to get down to brass tacks, no pun intended."

I pause. And grin right back.

Santosha means "acceptance." One of the **niyamas, santosha** is a guideline for relating to ourselves. *Santosha* invites a richness of acceptance and love into our relationships by giving both parties the space to be as they truly are. As you cultivate greater intimacy with another person, your expectations about who they should be can begin to dissolve in the light of who they actually are. Paradoxically, when we "give up hope" that something will be different, the tapestry and richness of the current moment can bloom because we are not trying to change ourselves—or our partners—to be liked.

When your sense of self is healthy, you glow.

When you trust who you are, you can be fully expressive with another person, because you don't have to pretend to be something that you are not. When you trust that you are okay, you allow yourself to be seen without fear of rejection.

The opportunity: practice courage. Don't settle for a safe, tepid, and sterile interaction with a potential partner—or with anyone. You are loveable for your wonderful uniqueness, your colorfulness, and your unexpected corners.

And the right person will love you for those details.

FAITH

Being courageous requires faith.

My mom is rolling her eyes. "Oh, it *was that nurse.*"

My dad pipes up from the kitchen, "Oh c'mon, Cheryl."

My mom whispers, "He dated her when he thought we had broken up."

My dad has good ears. "We *had* broken up!"

"Didn't you date other guys, too?" I ask my mom pointedly. "When you guys were on your, uh, off-time?"

Mom assumes an expression of utter innocence.

"Yes," says my dad loudly, "*couple of bozos.*"

My parents were high school sweethearts. There are photos of him accompanying her to her senior prom. Dad, a skinny basketball player; Mom, a gorgeous debutante.

My mother rolls her eyes, dismissing Dad's outrage. "Well, we were off and on in college, and then we were really apart when your dad was in the Marine Corps. But then we decided that we wanted to be with each other." She nods and smiles at my father. "And so, we got back together. And here we are."

My parents risked taking time apart, trusting that the right path for them would appear. And despite the nurse and the bozos, they chose to come back together.

If it's meant to be, it'll be. *Faith* is the process of trusting the unfolding.

Shraddha means "faith." *Shraddha* invites us to remember that we are participating in a much larger universal unfolding. We are limited in our human experience; we can't possibly control the world or know the future. Faith allows us to soften to the adventure and trust that everything will turn out as it is supposed to.

When we like someone, resting in uncertainty becomes very challenging. We feel as if everything could dissolve in a moment! We want to control the situation to make sure that the outcome is what we want. We want to look good, be perfect, and make sure that there is a happy ending to our fairy tale.

When we start falling in love, we can get scared that our future with someone will hinge on a small detail. We feel mortified about our inelegant stumble or accidentally snorting our drink. We get paranoid that the entirety of the relationship will be destroyed when we blurt out that horrible secret that we never tell anyone (*do they think I'm a totally crazy now?!?!*).

But it won't.

The future success of your relationship won't hinge on the terribly awkward sex moment, your first fight, your inadvertent diss of his or her mom, or the first time that you fart really loudly.

When someone likes you—just as when you like someone else— they will like you for more than your details. There is a totality to who you are: your values, your voice, your sense of humor, and your attitude about life. In the face of your totality, the small stuff simply won't matter.

And here's the thing: the real you is going to come out eventually. Inevitably. So why hide?

Think of your past as your own personal iceberg.

To every interaction, you are bringing the significant weight of your experience, actions, and life. While your behavior (the tip of the iceberg) is on view for the world, it's really the weight of all the unseen ice underneath (your history) that dictates where the iceberg goes.

Karma is the residue of the action that we have taken. In short, we have baggage, and (unless he or she is enlightened) your date has baggage too. Our lives are continually unfolding within a larger tapestry of action. And even though we strive for self-awareness, we are also directed by subconscious forces that aren't always in our control. Our work is to be in the moment and do our best.

The other person has a similarly weighty history. When you go on a date, you are only able to see the tip of his or her iceberg. The rest remains hidden.

But over time, the iceberg will be revealed. And chances are that there will be some interesting surprises in what lies beneath. Though we may try to pretty-up the topside (look, I put a Christmas tree on my iceberg, ta-da!), changing the superficial landscape ultimately won't change the deeper terrain. Eventually, the navigation of your iceberg will reveal the contours of what lies beneath the water.

So why not be authentic from the start and save yourself the time of all the pretending?

Literally meaning "without color," *vairagya* means non-attachment. Non-attachment is not the same thing as not caring; we can care deeply but also stay rooted in our inner, intrinsic wholeness so that we can experience the world without being so reactive.

When we begin to edit out who we are because we are afraid that we don't match up with someone—when we try to be *liked* rather than be ourselves—then we're postponing the inevitable reveal. And in the meantime, we're depriving ourselves of the opportunity to be fully self-expressive—and depriving our dates of the opportunity to experience us as we authentically are.

Faith means remembering that if it's meant to be, then you will both jump over the awkward hurdles of texting, protocol, and embarrassment in order to step closer. "Success" is not all on your shoulders. Your person will meet you halfway. Your person will want to walk beside you.

If it's meant to be, it will be.

"One doesn't discover new lands without consenting to lose sight of the shore for a very long time."
—André Gide, *The Counterfeiters*

PRACTICES

Journal: Self-Trust

- How do you want people to see you? Why? What happens if they don't?

- What secrets do you have? Why are they secrets? What would it feel like if you told them to someone?

- What qualities do you hide? Are you hiding them because you would really like to change them, or because you are afraid of what people think?

Dating Practice: Trust

- Notice when you feel anxious in a dating relationship, or when you feel a desire to be liked rather than seen for who you are. Explore your fear: what are you afraid of? What's the worst thing that could happen?

- Notice when you stifle yourself (don't say what you think, what you feel, or otherwise edit yourself). Where did the impulse to edit come from? And how did it make you feel?

- Notice when you feel like yourself: free, expressive, and unedited. What created those circumstances?

Meditation Practice: Wholeness

Yoga reminds us that we are already whole, perfect, and free. For this meditation, choose one word (mantra) that empowers your full sense of self. For example, "beauty," "whole," "surrender," or "magnificent."

- Find your meditation seat (see chapter two for more detailed instructions if needed).

- Follow your breath.

- On each inhale and exhale, repeat your chosen mantra.

- After about five minutes, take a few normal breaths.

- Sense how you feel.

Yoga Practice: Trust

- Tree

- Eagle

As you explore these balancing poses, change your point of view. Rather than resist their inherent shakiness, embrace it as an opportunity to "learn to fall." If you feel steady, close your eyes. Recognize that the fear of falling is simply a fear; we have lost nothing.

Chapter 11
ECSTASY

Pleasure. Say it.

Pleasure.

It sounds naughty, decadent, and absolutely delicious.

You have the right to feel pleasure. You have the right to feel marvelous in your skin and to enjoy the bounty of sensations that are available to you through your senses in every moment. You have the right to experience your body as the gift of your aliveness. It's your door prize for admission onto the planet.

So many of us deprive ourselves of the sensory feast that is right at our fingertips. More than ever, today's world encourages us to live in our heads rather than our bodies. We connect virtually to our friends, jobs, and the world. Our lives are mediated through the internet, our computers, and our various e-devices. We sit at desks, drive in cars, and export our consciousness to the cloud. Everyday interactions are digital rather than organic.

Sensual experience is a powerful opportunity to get out of the virtual world and come back home to your body and yourself.

You can enjoy the richness of your body's capacity to feel through your skin, your muscles, and your bones. Pleasure immerses you immediately in the present moment and awakens you to the very core of your aliveness.

However, while pleasure is an intrinsic part of being human, yoga and sex haven't always been friends.

Let's look at why.

A Brief History of Sex and Yoga

When yoga began more than three thousand years ago, it was not the physical practice that we know and love today. (Some scholars believe yoga is more than five thousand years old. Opinions vary.) Practicing yoga meant meditating; yogis believed that enlightenment was found by looking inwards. The external, physical world—full of sensual distractions such as food, drink, and sex—was an impediment to this spiritual journey.

When we desire something, we usually can't help thinking about it, which makes it hard for our minds to settle down.

For example, in the morning, I am a barely human creature consumed by a desire for Starbucks coffee so fervent that I can think of little else until I get it.

To avoid these distractions, ye olden yogis chose to be ascetics who avoided worldly pleasures. They would fast and practice celibacy. Many of us have experienced the waning of desire that renunciation can bring. For example, when we go on a dietary cleanse, we are often giving up something we enjoy. After a period of adaptation, we usually start to accept that we can't eat the pound cake in the fridge, and we don't think about it as much anymore. But once a forbidden item is back on the menu, our minds start murmuring their cravings again.

Sex is the mack daddy of sensual delights.

Think about it: when you are attracted to someone, how distracted does your mind get?

When I am attracted to someone, the object of my affection starts to take up pretty much all of my conscious real estate. It's as if the hamsters in my brain have decided to watch a movie marathon of every romantic comedy ever produced. With good reason, yogis considered this distraction an obstacle to meditation. And to avoid this trouble, they practiced celibacy (*brahmacharya*) and took sex entirely off the menu.

Don't panic.

I promise you that you don't have to take a vow of celibacy to be a good yogi. Lucky for us, in the Middle Ages, a yoga philosophy called tantra offered a new point of view that revolutionized the way that we could relate to the sensual delights of the world.

When you hear the word "tantra," you may have a hazy image of Sting, sex, and the *Kama Sutra*, so let's look a little deeper.

While there are many branches of tantra, we're going to talk about a branch of tantra that subscribes to *nondualism*. Nondualism proposes that the material world (*prakriti*, the realm of your Little Self) and the spiritual world (*purusha,* the realm of your Big Self) aren't really separate. In fact, the divine is embodied through the physical manifestation of the world. Another way of saying this is that God (however you might define God) isn't separate from us. The world is God incarnate.

So rather than avoiding the material world because it is a distraction on the road to enlightenment, the world around us can be experienced as the unfolding expression of divinity itself.

Whoa. Let's take that again. Slowly.

The world is the unfolding expression of divinity itself.

In other words, we don't have to *avoid* the world in order to become enlightened. Everything in the whole universe—including us!—is sacred. From this point of view, nothing in the material world is inherently bad.

According to tantric philosophy, we—through our bodies (and feelings, thoughts, and relationships)—are participating in the continually unfolding expression of the universe.

With this transformation of thought, the entire landscape of human physical experience—including our sexuality—becomes an opportunity for spiritual connection. Rather than being an impediment to our spiritual evolution, our senses can be our tools for self-realization.

Pretty awesome.

Tantra is a branch of philosophy that upholds a non-dual view of the universe. "Non-dual" means that there is no true separation between the divine and the material. The world is an unfolding expression of Universal Consciousness in a multiplicity of forms. Therefore, rather than transcending the world, we can experience rapture *through* the world. Yay!

The physical yoga practice that you know and love has emerged from tantra's generous bosom. Through your yoga practice, you are using your body as a vehicle for self-transformation. So, whether you knew it or not before this moment, you, my friend, are doing a tantric practice every time you unroll your yoga mat.

Now, a note about Hitler and other bad people.

When I wrote, "from this point of view, nothing within the material world is inherently bad," some of you may rightfully have perked up as you considered some of the crappy things that happen in the world. You may have thought, "Hey, those things are bad! Not everything that happens in the world is good!"

Yes, here is the conundrum of non-dual philosophy: if everything in the world is part of the divine, then why does bad stuff happen? Isn't God all good?

Some philosophies create the "devil" or "evil" to explain away the stuff in the world that we don't like. However, tantra takes a slightly different approach. While tantra would say that "everything is God" from the very *highest* perspective, not everything will seem okay (or is okay) from our human perspective.

Let's return for a moment to our virtual reality metaphor. If life is truly the ultimate virtual reality game, then nothing that happens in the game is really that terrible—when seen and understood from the perspective of the Big Self. However, for the Little Self, who is immersed in the virtual reality, the bad shit can definitely feel well, like bad shit. Because it is.

Understanding the larger perspective doesn't mean that we become apathetic about the fate of the world. The world is a reflection of the divine and—as we explored in chapter four—we are the architects of creation.

But here's the riddle: in the tantric worldview, no one is holding a gun to our heads and threatening us with punishment or damnation if we are bad. Instead, we make choices that align with our values because we can, and because we want to, as an expression of our own creative power. We are responsible. We are being good people because we want to uphold our own values—not because anyone is "making us." We make our virtual reality what it is.

Life is a game. And we can choose to play it well.

Now let's talk about sex.

HONOR YOUR FEELINGS

I was a late bloomer. Nerdy, flat-chested, and sporting a mouth full of braces,

I was far more comfortable fantasizing about the men in my sister's romance novels than dealing with the goofy teenage boys skulking around my high school.

Keenly aware that I was lagging behind my gal pals in real-world experience, I believed that I could learn everything I needed to know about "making out" if I did enough academic research. I grilled my girlfriends relentlessly for data:

- "When he kisses you, how do you turn your head?"

- "How does your tongue move, is it like sweeping, or is more of an in-and-out thing?"

- "Where do you put your hands? Shoulders, back? Do you move them?"

As you can surmise, my first kiss was a disaster of intellectualism. In my perfectionist quest to "do it right," I did not feel a thing.

I'd finally cornered my teenage crush (Geoff, yes, Geoff! The love child of C. Thomas Howell and Robert Sean Leonard! The boy of my dreams!) in my bedroom. On my rainbow-colored waterbed, to be exact. He was no longer dating Laura, the sporty senior, and was free to smooch other ladies.

"If I could have anyone be my first kiss, I'd want it to be you," I say breathlessly.

"Well," he clears his throat. "You'd have to take your glasses off."

Oh my God, is this really happening? I whip my glasses off (which, uh, duh, you actually don't need to do) and toss them aside. Then I face off like a kissing gladiator.

He leans in. His lips touch mine. They're soft. And then, oh my God, he licks my lips and sticks his tongue into my mouth. Now, I've been prepped for this maneuver, so I think that I should turn my head. But dammit, his tongue is moving around, and now that I'm here, I have no idea what to do with it. It feels big and wet. Do I suck on it? Duel with it?

I have no idea how long this lasts, but I have a vague sense that what is happening is not sexy *at all*.

When he pulls back, I feel like an octopus has just landed on my face. "Um. Huh. I think I'm a sloppy kisser," I say. I wonder where my glasses are.

"I think you're perfect," he says stoutly, surreptitiously wiping away some of my drool. He really is a sweetheart.

My confusion with sensuality did not get better over time.

Sex—when it finally happened—was almost shockingly disappointing. For me, it was indeed an "act" rather than an "experience." I couldn't reconcile the "heaving, throbbing" rapture that I had read about in my novels with the pushy, inept, alienating experience that I was having with my boyfriend.

His name was Mikey, by the way. Geoff and I had reverted to being "just friends" after our kissing adventure. Mikey was a smart kid who wore an earring (scandalous!), worked as a DJ, and looked like Waldo from *Where's Waldo*.

Mikey was my first real boyfriend. And while he was a nice enough guy, it turns out that I had a real problem communicating my feelings and boundaries to him. And, unfortunately, my challenge in communicating extended to my ability to talk about having—or not having—sex. I did not know how to say, "No, this doesn't feel right." When difficult feelings surfaced ("difficult" being any feelings that might be at odds with what Mikey wanted at the time), I felt as if there were a giant hand around my throat. I simply couldn't speak.

I wound up performing my way through sex. I acted in a way that I thought looked good. Despite the distinct lack of "pulsating waves of pleasure," I kept having sex with Mikey in the hopes that my experience would change. And I thought (again with the thinking, thinking, thinking!) that I had an obligation to meet his expectations. God forbid he was disappointed.

With Mikey, I had sex because I thought I *should*, not because I wanted to. I started to hate sex. I started to hate Mikey, too. And I hid all of these confusing feelings beneath a happy face. Poor Mikey had no idea of the icy rage that was coiled in the figure beneath him.

"Should" is sex's death knell.

Many of us have had sex when it didn't feel right. Comedian Amy Schumer darkly jests, "We've all been a little raped." Rape is not funny; her joke speaks to the terrible prevalence of non-consensual sex. Some of us have had undesired sex forced upon us. Others (like me) have forced *ourselves* into it somehow. Exploring rape is far beyond the scope of my expertise; I acknowledge it here because the sad fact is that many of us have had negative sexual experiences. Listening to our bodies and honoring what we truly want is essential for nourishing and reclaiming a whole sense of self.

Even those of us who have been blessed with a happy sexual history have probably had sex when something didn't feel right or was "off." To fully enjoy the richness of sex, we must stop our fragmentation and bring the heart, head, and body together in our decision and experience.

By upholding our right to make an integrated choice, we leave no part of ourselves on the sidelines.

"THE RULES"

Have you heard of the "Third Date Rule?"

Someone, somewhere decided that you shouldn't have sex until the third date. Apparently, three is the magic number. If you wait till the third date, then you're not too easy, but you're also not a holdout. Hundreds of books have been written about the "code" of sexual conduct and dating (do this, but don't do that!). It's like a terrible continuation of my relentless note-taking as a teenager when I was trying to figure out how to kiss a guy. We look for "the answer" that will help us determine the "right" way to act.

Bullshit.

Here's the thing: there are no rules to dictate when or when not to kiss, have sex, or let someone touch your bare belly. Your choice is your choice. And the right person will be cool with *whatever* you decide. Some people don't want to have sex until they're married; others are comfortable with sex from first sight. There is no right or wrong here, and there is no magic formula to follow. You are not a slut; you are not frigid. If any of these kinds of judgments are getting thrown around, then they are coming from someone who lacks the empathy to understand you and be your person.

Acting with integrity means that our mind, body, and emotions are united in moving forward with what we are doing.

Any external rules that we try to follow will actually take us further from our own insight and wisdom.

The only rule you need to follow? Trust yourself. This means that if sex doesn't feel right, you get to say no.

Saying No

The voice of "no" can be quiet and is frequently drowned out by a cacophony of chatter from the mind. How many of us have eaten when we are not hungry, had sex when we weren't interested, or pushed through our physical limits when we were sick and should have been in bed? The body's wisdom can easily be trampled by the ego's agenda.

To become integrated, we must pause and listen to what our body is saying. *Practice the pause.* By taking a moment to breathe, feel, and move into the space beyond our thoughts, we can practice honoring what our body really wants. When we can hear what we need, then we can make a more informed choice that upholds our whole experience.

Ojas is our primal sense of vigor and fundamental energy reserve. *Ojas* is fed through our senses, experience, and the food that nourishes our bodies. When we have sex, *ojas* is said to be depleted. Conserving our own vital energy gives us permission to choose which experiences enliven and feed us and which experiences are unsatisfying or detracting. We are given full permission to protect our sensual and sexual experience: are we being nourished or depleted?

Remember Ethan from Tinder?

After we moved past the initial confusion over mixed signals and paying for checks, we started dating. An engineer and a sailor, he took me on summer evening cruises where we grilled salmon, watched the sunset, and drank cold white wine. He was well informed, adventurous, and enough of a geek to be totally sexy. He was patient, laid back, and we took things slow.

After a couple of months, I felt that it might be time to sleep over at Ethan's apartment. I arrived on our date with toothbrush and birth control in tow. However, despite the preparation, there was something that didn't feel quite right in our chemistry. My mind was full of exasperated chatter: "Don't be a tease," "Why not just do it?" "Don't disappoint him," "You've come this far!"

I have an old, dogged habit of being afraid of disappointing men. From my very first sexual experience, I've made their expectations more important than my experience. And here I was, nearly forty, with those same voices chattering in my ear.

But I didn't want to listen to them anymore.

I pause. I try to get quiet, ignore my crazy mind chatter, and really listen to my body.

I'm not feeling it.

"I'm sorry," I say finally. "I'm not there yet."

He props himself up and looks at me. "This doesn't just ... drive you crazy?"

It seems impolite to say, "Uh, no, which is why I'd rather just go to sleep."

"I know, I wish I were," I'm sincere in this wish. I'd rather be caught up in an unfettered, animal display of passion than having this particular conversation. "But I'm just not there yet."

"Seriously?" He sounds surprised.

"Um, yeah, seriously."

He lays back in silence.

The silence grows.

I start to get that tight feeling in my chest. It's the feeling that says, "I'm bad, I've done something wrong." It's the feeling that I'll do just about anything to avoid.

I frown up at the ceiling. Fuck that feeling.

"I'm leaving," I suddenly say. My body says "no," and I am going. For the first time in my life, I am going to leave someone's bed. Even though it seems rude.

"I'm sorry, this just doesn't feel good. I'm going home." I pack up my things—toothbrush, birth control, and all—and I go.

Soon thereafter, Ethan told me that he had been having feelings for another woman.

Perhaps a deep inner sixth sense had steered me to wait on intimacy, or perhaps I was simply lucky with my timing. Either way, I was happy that I had listened to my intuition.

The right person wants the relationship to work both ways. The right person will never mind waiting until the time is right for you.

Navigating the waters of sex and dating gives us the opportunity to reclaim the wildish intelligence of our bodies and emotions. We give this intelligence space to be held, nourished, and heard. The body does not speak the same language as the mind: its logic and timing are different. When we reclaim and validate our body's wordless and inchoate intuition, we affirm our wholeness and our trustworthiness. We can say, "I don't know why, but this doesn't feel right." We can trust our own truth.

That evening with Ethan, I listened to my feelings rather than following the rules. Rather than doing what I thought I *should*, I listened to my instincts. My whole body. My full self. And because I did, I took care of myself.

SAYING YES

When we trust ourselves to say no, we can also trust ourselves to say yes.

At first, Alex and I had decided that we should be friends rather than pursue a relationship. I was too afraid of his history with alcoholism to commit to something more. But we loved hanging out with each other. As we earned each other's trust, the sexual tension between us started ramping up.

My mind pulled back. "It's not appropriate," it said primly to my restless and burning body. "You are friends now, you are not dating. You can't go down that road. It's not right. It's not safe." So I kept my hands to myself. Or at least, I tried.

One cold fall day, Alex and I went to a lecture at a local college. Partway through the talk, Alex rested his hand on my back. I started burning up. The speaker probably gave us the answer to the human condition. I have no idea. I missed every word.

With Alex, I was still fighting my body's intuition, but this time my instincts were saying "yes" rather than "no." My mind was trying to keep me safe by following the "rules," but the problem was that I was ignoring what I really wanted.

I wanted him.

I drop him off at his place after the lecture.

"I didn't hear any of that lecture," I blurt out.

"You didn't?"

"No. I didn't hear a word."

"Me neither." He grins wolfishly, and leans in to kiss me.

"No, no, wait!" I scramble. "No, we agreed that this is not a good idea."

"We said? No, *you* said. I'm all for it."

"We decided to be friends," I say stoutly. "Friends. Friends do not have sexual relations."

"Why not?"

I ignore him. "And it won't work because ... Well, there are so many reasons ..."

Even while I'm talking about pulling away, I start to feel my body lean into his. I pull back and press myself into my car door determinedly.

He rolls his eyes at me and sighs. "You know, all this time that you've been talking, we could have been making out already."

"Out of the car. I'm going home."

I drive home, alone, stewing. In my own juices, so to speak.

In my apartment, I pace around restlessly. Getting involved with Alex sexually was such a bad idea. Wasn't it?

His history with alcoholism, my history with alcoholics. Bad, bad idea. No relationship there. Bad road to travel. Sure, my body felt like it was on fire, but sex would just make things complicated.

I pull up short in sudden realization.

Things were already complicated between us. Not having sex wasn't changing any of that. It was obvious that I was conflicted and sending out mixed signals.

"Complicated" wasn't why I was hesitating.

I was scared because I didn't think I could trust myself.

I had a history of being afraid of disappointing others. Wary of anger and conflict, I silenced myself to keep the peace. While this habit wasn't that problematic when it meant avoiding a verbal fight, it became insidious when I was afraid of disappointing sexual partners.

My mind was trying to protect me from getting myself into a situation that would spiral into obligation and self-betrayal. I was afraid that—if I followed through on my sexual desire for Alex—I would trap myself in a situation where I felt obligated, silenced, and ultimately disempowered.

But I *had* earned my own trust. I was no longer the girl who wouldn't leave a bad situation. After all, hadn't I proven that during my experience with Ethan? I had become someone who would listen to my own body, honor my feelings, break the rules, and leave—if I had to—in the middle of the night.

I didn't need to live according to my fears. I was already safe. I had trusted myself to say no. And now I could trust myself to say yes.

With this new realization, I was willing to change my mind. I got back into my car and drove to Alex's apartment.

Let's just say that he was happy to see me.

RESPONSIBILITY

Wanting sex is normal.

Once upon a time, there was a chariot being pulled by five horses named Smell, Sight, Hearing, Taste, and Touch. These are the senses. Excited by everything around them, those horses ran willy-nilly after whatever new and delicious experience came across their path. Carrots! Rabbits! Hay! Their tendency to race around didn't make them bad horses; it was simply their nature to chase after yummy things. At the reins was a charioteer (the mind). When the charioteer wasn't paying attention, the horses would run everywhere. But when the charioteer was present and awake, the horses could be steered.

However, the chariot only really got where it was supposed to go when the charioteer listened to the passenger sitting in the chariot. When the mind listened to the passenger (the Big Self), then the chariot found its way to its destination.

—Classical Hindu story, adapted from the *Katha Upanishad*

In this story, the horses are our senses, the charioteer is our mind, and the passenger is our soul.

Raga means "attraction" and is a natural attachment to pursuing objects that bring us pleasure. When we become overly attached to the objects of our senses (whether it's food, drink, sex, drugs) or try to use them to solve our problems, pleasure has become dysfunctional craving.

Despite some indoctrination to the contrary, we (humans) actually like pleasure. When we accept the nature of our senses, we don't have the unrealistic expectation that they aren't going to crave stuff. Accepting our nature allows us to get out of the blame cycle ("Why do I want this?" "I can't control myself!") and allows us to do the real work of taking responsibility for guiding our horses with more mastery.

As yogis, we have a responsibility to respect the power of pleasure and use it wisely. When we experience craving, loneliness, anger, or sadness, our first temptation is often to use something pleasurable—like sex—to cover these feelings up. We drink the wine and text the guy, not because we really want to do those things, but because we're trying to make the *bad feelings* go away. And it works—temporarily.

We often use pleasure as a Band-Aid for the Missing Piece, rather than allowing ourselves to experience our real feelings.

When Alex and I broke up, I spent many evenings alone in my small apartment, desperate to use alcohol and food to distract myself from the pain of our separation. An epic battle occurred every night over the wine bottle. I knew it would be better to meditate, read, or practice yoga, but I wanted nothing more than to glug a glass and bury myself in Netflix. I won't lie: many nights the wine won. But when I used wine or food to cover up my feelings, I just felt worse.

Pain can't be healed by pleasure; it can only be healed by Presence, compassion, and time. And when I used pleasure to cover up my pain, I was starving myself of what I really needed to heal. It was like eating sugar when I needed vegetables.

Using pleasure to cover up our Missing Piece disrespects the power of our senses. Wine is delicious; popcorn is a treat. However, by turning these pleasures into painkillers, I undermined the sacredness of their offering.

When we find ourselves seeking pleasure, it's time again to *practice the pause.* Why do we really want it? Are we using it to escape or cover up our pain?

When we realize that we are using pleasure as a cover up, then we can take a breath and do the hard, spiritual work of sitting with our feelings rather than avoiding them. And if we truly want the yummy thing because it's a great time for a treat, then we are able to enjoy it.

Brahmacharya is "celibacy." A yogic guideline for living, *brahmacharya* describes the practice of chastity. However, as non-celibate yogic practitioners, **brahmacharya** can be seen as an invitation for mindful sensuality. Are we trapped by sensual pleasure, or can we experience the sensuality of the world without fear, attachment, or over-indulgence? **Brahmacharya** is an invitation to an open inquiry and search for moderation and accountability in our experience.

When we trust ourselves to deal with our feelings, then we can trust that we aren't using pleasure as a cop out. We can enjoy pleasure purely for its own sake, freely and fully. Sex becomes an affirmation of our humanity; an explosion of experience; and a ridiculous romp through all the shivers, tingles, and delight that our magnificent human body has to offer. What a glorious experience to share with another human!

"The wise prefer the good to the pleasant, but the unwise choice the pleasant through love of bodily pleasure."
—Katha Upanishad

We often confuse pleasure for happiness, but they are not the same. Pleasure is a temporary sensual state. Delightful as it is, it will only be truly satisfying when we enjoy it in integrity with our hearts and minds.

And just as importantly, we can take pleasure—and we can leave it. Reducing our dependence on pleasure is essential for having a healthy relationship. After all, we do not have sex alone. Just as you have the right to say yes and no, so does your partner. When we aren't attached to using sex as an ego booster, power trip, or Band-Aid, then we can be with our partners more fully. When we're not attached to a pleasurable outcome, then we can offer our partners the gracious space to make their own best choice regarding sex—without the pressure of disappointing us.

WHOLENESS

Relishing your sensuality—and your sexuality—is a process of self-trust: trusting that you have the capacity to experience the wild, tumultuous, and exuberant oceans of cravings, sensations, and feelings responsibly and with grace.

Bringing a yogic mindset to your sensuality is not about dulling or restraining your experience. Rather, it's about evolving your mindfulness and care to the point that you can feel more, experience more, and express more—but with an equal measure of compassion, respect, and responsibility. With such awareness, you can trust that you won't compromise yourself or someone else in the process. You can enjoy pleasure without dilution, shame, or doubt.

Sexuality is about far more than just sex; it's a reflection of your relationship to your *sensuality*. While sex is an occasional act, you are perpetually immersed in the world of your senses. It's time to practice coming home to our bodies and ourselves.

Svadhishthana chakra

Our second energy center located in the pelvis, **svadhishthana** is the locus of our sensuality, fluidity, and deep emotion. When the energy center is well balanced, we experience our sexuality freely and intuitively, generously and with integrity. The element associated with **svadhishthana** is water, indicating that feelings and sensuality have a natural ebb and flow, inviting us to experience our emotions and feelings while recognizing their inherent transitory nature.

Opportunities to nourish your senses are ever-present! Eat one meal exquisitely slowly and savor what you taste. Take a walk through the woods and see the individual colors of the trees. Enjoy the texture of a cashmere sweater or a cat's soft fur. Read lush poetry and taste each word. Take a deep breath and luxuriate in the sensation of expansion and space. In tantra, this respectful delight in your senses is called "feeding the gods."

"We must increase our capacity for pleasure."
—My anatomy and dissection teacher, the wonderful Gil Hedley

Practice your wholesome *sensuality*. Own your pleasure. And share it with wonder, respect, and delight.

PRACTICES

Life Practice: Awakening

This practice is designed to bring us "back" to our senses throughout our day. Set a timer to go off each hour. (A timer on your phone or an app can be used to set intervals.) When you are pinged by your timer, stop and do a "sense inventory." This may include:

- Feeling the pleasure of breathing and feeling your lungs stretch

- Smelling your coffee

- Tasting your food

- Hearing the sounds around you

- Seeing the colors around you.

Most of the time, we rush past these everyday delicacies. This simple practice connects you instantly to your body, and you will also notice that each hour brings you something different.

Dating Practice: Delight Your Senses

If you already have a partner, explore the sensual feast at your fingertips. Rather than rushing to sex, take the time to explore the sensual possibilities of taste, touch, smell, and sound. Exquisitely linger.

If you are on a date, give yourself the time and space to experience this person through the lens of your senses. How does this person smell, sound? What do you feel in your own body when you are around him or her?

Meditation Practice: Nourish Your Senses

Select a sense to focus on: sound, taste, sight, sensation, smell. Although I will use sound in this particular guidance, you can choose a different sense each time you do this practice. Do this slowly the first time (take about five minutes). Once you get the hang of "tuning in," you can take a few moments at any time in your day to connect to your senses more deeply.

- Find your meditation seat (see chapter two for more detailed instructions if needed).

- Close your eyes in order to refine your awareness.

- Begin by hearing the sounds around you.

- What is the texture of the sound, the rhythm? How does the vibration feel?

- Allow yourself to hear the sounds arise and fall away.

- After a little while, expand your awareness to include sounds that are far away.

- Hear the sounds arise and fall without expectation.

- Let go of the need to identify the sounds and give yourself permission to hear without labeling sounds as "good" or "bad."

- Sit in the spaciousness of the field of sound.

- Begin to feel your own Presence, hearing the sounds as they arise.

- Become aware of your sense of hearing, tuning you into each vibration.

- Pause. Ask: Who is hearing?

- After a few minutes, take a few deep breaths and open your eyes.

- Does the world feel any different?

Yoga Practice: Sensual Experience

- Lizard

- Saddle

Hip openers are famously linked to our deep, sensual and emotional centers. As you explore these poses, consider: how could your yoga practice feel 10–15% more delicious in your body? Rather than treat your yoga practice as something to "perform," use your yoga practice as a tool to connect to the pleasure of moving your body and feeling your breath. How does your practice change if this is your priority?

Chapter 12
BATTLE

I've always been afraid of conflict.

I associate the word "conflict" with violence, irrationality, anger, and fear. Not only does conflict scare the pants off me, but it also seems at odds with the yogic principle of compassionate nonviolence (*ahimsa*).

As you might imagine, my ideas about conflict have led to a few problems. Afraid of saying something that might disappoint or anger my partner, I have pre-emptively avoided possible confrontation by shutting down and withdrawing into silence. I have turned relationships into prisons where I felt silenced and constrained.

During my marriage, I rode this self-annihilation train to its last stop.

"I'm going to start drinking again," my husband says in our ship's cabin.

"What?" I say.

"I'm going to start drinking again. Just for a while. Just for this trip."

I freeze.

My husband and I are on an Alaskan cruise for our honeymoon. We chose to get married during our great emigration from New York City to Vancouver, British Columbia.

However, the day before our wedding, his mother had unexpectedly died. He had found her body. They had been very close. He was devastated.

"You want to drink for the cruise," I ask.

"I need to."

My husband has been dry for ten years. He is the kind of guy who spits out chocolates with liqueur.

There is a long moment. "Can I say anything to change your mind?" I say at last.

"No."

"Can you at least go to the Bill W. meeting first? They have them here. Go to a meeting first and then decide?" Bill W. is code for Alcoholics Anonymous.

He pauses, nods slowly. "Yeah, I can do that. But it's not going to change my mind."

"Okay. Just go," I say.

He goes.

I wait.

He returns.

"They said I should do it."

"Drink."

"Yeah, when I told them what happened. How I felt. Just for this cruise."

"They said you should drink?" I am shocked. The world tilts.

"Yes."

"... Just for the cruise. And then you'll stop?"

"Yeah," he nods. "It's just to get through this."

Five months later, we are sitting in a bar in Vancouver.

"Could you ..." I stop and begin again. He's looking at me. "... Maybe you could just stop at ... three beers? Or maybe say, four?"

I know he's an alcoholic. Deep down, he knows *he's* an alcoholic. Yet, here we are. In Canada, across a bar table, staring at each other.

He laughs, and it's not a very nice laugh. He looks down. "You know, you are so selfish."

Am I? I think. *Am I being selfish?*

"I know you think you're being reasonable, but you just don't get it." He starts getting angry. "Everyone drinks. It's not a problem."

I shrink. "Yes, but, you ... you're ..."

"No. Everyone drinks."

I am out of my depth. I hate myself for not knowing what to do. I have no solution: I feel deeply, sickly wrong when I don't protest his drinking and then am attacked when I do.

I have become the codependent wife of an alcoholic.

He sits back in his chair. "Just when I think you're being supportive, you say something like that. You are so selfish."

I feel something enormous rising inside of me that I don't recognize. It's a strange beast that I cannot name nor place. Although I don't know what it is in that moment, much later I realize that it is anger.

I shove the feeling down, and it curdles into self-hatred. I am silent.

I am afraid of being yelled at, afraid of being a bad person, afraid of being alone, afraid of making someone upset, afraid of uncertainty, and afraid of backing out of a commitment.

It's easy now to look back and shake my head. "Why didn't you just leave? Speak up? Yell back? Draw a line?"

Because—most of all—I was afraid of being selfish.

SELFISH

"You're so selfish."

Was I?

"Selfish" is a loaded word. It's awful. When my husband called me selfish, my arguments withered. I recoiled so violently from the word "selfish" that I never questioned what it actually meant.

Because here was the trap: he was right. I was selfish.

But here was *my* confusion: being selfish wasn't bad.

When my husband called me "selfish," he was really saying, "You're acting a certain way, but I want you to do something else, so I'm going to call you selfish and shame you emotionally so that I can have my way instead."

Isn't that also ... well ... selfish?

I'm not sure what led to the turning point. Likely it was a combination of the emotional abuse, disconnected sex, and failed therapy. One night ten months into my marriage—after a particularly bad fight—I found myself in the kitchen, cutting my arm with one of our kitchen knives.

I stopped and looked down at the cuts, welling with blood. I found him in our bedroom.

"I'm cutting myself again." I hadn't cut myself since high school when I used scissors to exorcise my displaced feelings of anger, desperation, and anxiety.

He didn't look at me. "Now you know how it feels."

I stepped back in alarm. I looked at my arm. While I could selectively ignore my *emotional* decline, I could not dismiss the quite obvious dysfunction of my *physical* actions. I was self-destructing. And my husband was so far into his own personal hell that he was happy to have me join him there. I realized in that moment that I could not stay with him. No matter how tragic his circumstances or his loss, I could not be with someone who thought it was A-OK for me to take a knife to my arm.

Enabling his drinking hadn't helped our marriage. Silencing my feelings had made things worse. Joining him in his personal hell wasn't going to help either one of us. I had become a shadow of my former self, and no one (not even my husband) was benefiting from this sad transformation.

That's when I left.

"The kindest thing we can do for everyone concerned is to know when to say 'enough.' Many people use Buddhist ideals to justify self-debasement. In the name of not shutting our heart, we let people walk all over us. It is said that in order not to break our vow of compassion we have to learn when to stop aggression and draw the line. There are times when the only way to bring down the barriers is to set boundaries."
—Pema Chödrön, *The Places That Scare You*

In my marriage, I suffered from a great confusion: I thought that self-interest was bad and that loving someone else meant being a doormat. Because of this confusion, I mistook codependence and enabling for support. Only when I had been stripped down to my emotional bones and was cowering in a deep corner inside myself did I finally say, "Is this enough?" When I left, I recognized that I could not make him better by making myself smaller; giving up my strength did not mean that he would gain his.

It was time to learn to deal with conflict.

CONFLICT

Having an honest, authentic, and intimate relationship is going to require you to deal with conflict. There is no getting around it. At some point, someone is going to sulk about sex, forget to wash the dishes, or reach their wits' end with a screaming kid. Being a good yogi isn't about "nama-staying out of the fire," but about learning to navigate these moments with clarity and compassion.

You may be surprised to know that the yogis have thought long and hard about conflict. The art of war is exquisitely explored in the epic story of the *Bhagavad Gita* (the Lord's Song), one of India's most precious philosophical treasures. The *Bhagavad Gita* was Gandhi's favorite book, by the way. Makes sense, doesn't it? After all, it's hard to stand up to imperialism and injustice if you're not willing to jump into the fray.

"On the field of Truth, on the battlefield of Life, what came to pass, Sanjaya, when my sons and their warriors faced those of my brother Pandu?"
—The first line of the *Bhagavad Gita,*
translated by Juan Mascaro

Here's the story:

Our hero, Arjuna, is about to go to war with his own family. Before the battle, he gets into his chariot and rides out across the field. Across enemy lines, he sees his cherished friends and family members. Although Arjuna is on the right side of the law, he despairs over the futility of the impending violence. "No good can come from killing my own kinsmen in battle ... we should turn back from this evil." He throws down his weapons. He will not fight.

Arjuna begs his charioteer Krishna (God in disguise) for advice, which is Krishna's invitation to teach Arjuna the true meaning of yoga. Through Krishna's teachings, Arjuna realizes that practicing yoga isn't about sitting on the sidelines. Practicing yoga does not even necessarily mean nonviolence.

To practice yoga, Arjuna must follow his duty (*dharma*) and uphold his soul's purpose. Contrary to what he may prefer, he must fight.

The **Bhagavad Gita** is an epic story that describes a famous, ancient battle. The battle is a metaphor for the challenges that we experience every day. The **Bhagavad Gita** asks us to investigate how we can live a spiritual life in the real world. Our yoga practice does not occur high on a mountaintop away from the action; we are in the thick of our own battles, doing our best to live well in our daily lives. Yoga isn't about getting away from life and relationships: "Yoga is skill in action."

The *Bhagavad Gita* recognizes that the world—at least the world of the Little Self—is not peaceful. On the contrary, it is a battlefield. We are in love with our enemies, engaged in struggle, and often confused about what we should do.

While we may not literally be in a life or death battle with our relatives, we can all relate to a situation in which we feel the need to stand up to someone that we love. As good yogis, we face the same questions that Arjuna is facing: should we take action, or should we stay out of the fray? How can we hurt people we love? How can we fight with integrity?

Dharma is "duty," or your life's calling. Your *dharma* invites you to uphold your soul's highest mission. Arjuna is not fighting from a place of high emotion or self-righteousness; he is going to war because it is the *just* action to take. When we are gearing up for a fight, we need to ask ourselves if we are acting from a place of reactivity, or whether we are entering battle to uphold the highest good.

Arjuna is not choosing to fight because he is angry or reactive. He is *choosing* to engage in conflict—fully cognizant of the consequences—because it is the *highest* choice that he can make for his life's purpose. He is entering the fray to uphold justice and the greatest good.

When we are about to put on our armor and wade into battle in our relationships, we must first *practice the pause* and be clear about our intentions. Like Arjuna, we can ask ourselves if our actions are in alignment with the highest good.

Are we fighting for our egos, or are we fighting for a higher purpose?

Arjuna's story is our story. *The Bhagavad Gita* is a call for us to live our yoga *in our relationships* as best we can. Like Arjuna, our yoga is "skill in action." Our yoga isn't just for the mat; it's demonstrated in every interaction that we have with the world around us. Mindful conflict—when it's pursued to uphold our highest self or the greatest good—is an essential part of this process.

ANGER

Anger is a signpost that indicates when our needs—explicit or unspoken—aren't being met. When we're angry, the world feels out of alignment because we are not getting what we want.

I was very angry during my marriage. But because I was afraid of anger (my own as well as that of my husband), I turned my feelings into self-punishment rather than listening to them.

When understood and acted upon responsibly, anger can be directed toward clarification and purification. Anger is information that gives us clarity about when we need to stake our boundaries and protect what is ours. Anger can be a mama bear: fierce, righteous, and healing.

"Bitterness is like cancer. It eats upon the host. But anger is like fire. It burns it all clean."
—Maya Angelou

Manipura Chakra

Located at the solar plexus, **manipura chakra** is an energy center that is controlled by the element of fire and is related to willpower and transformation. **Manipura** controls how we assert the ego (our Little Self) in relation to the world. When someone has excessive energy in this chakra, they may be controlling, overbearing, and rigid. If they have too little energy, they may lack a sense of centered self and be overly accommodating. Physically, **manipura** is related to digestion, which uses fiery substances (acids) to transform external material into sustenance. Similarly, **manipura** relates to our ability to emotionally "digest" and process our experiences.

Anger is a powerful force that must be managed responsibly so that its blaze is cleansing rather than destructive. Anger is an informative signpost, not a justification for bad behavior. Most of the time, feelings need to be processed before we react. But conscious and accountable anger can be the energy we need to make positive change. Wildfires are sometimes necessary to burn away the underbrush and make way for new growth.

Tapas

"The willingness to endure intensity for the sake of transformation." Literally meaning "heat," **tapas** stokes our inner flame, steels our discipline, and moves purposefully into the direction of our dreams.

The fire reminds us that we have the power to slough off our old snakeskins and emerge clean and vibrant.

Fire has been a symbol of purification and sacrifice for thousands of years. In ancient yoga rituals, fire was used to send offerings to the gods. As yoga evolved, these external ceremonies became internal rituals of purification. In our yoga practice, we stoke the flames of our inner fire, *agni,* and control this energy for purposeful and transformational use.

And just as important, once anger has done its clarifying work, we practice *letting the anger go.* In practical terms, this means that you don't bring up past issues that have already been laid to rest. "Remember the time that you ..." Recognizing anger's power to clarify is far different than calling up and opening old wounds. The former is cauterization; the latter is pulling scabs.

In the *Bhagavad Gita*, Arjuna learns that there is a caveat to following his dharma. In order to practice yoga in action, Arjuna must remain unattached to the results of these actions. In other words, he has to let go. He must do his personal best to fulfill his duty but surrender his attachment to the outcome. We cannot control the world, only ourselves. And once the battle is fought, we let it go.

Anger is strong medicine. Used wisely, it heals. Used indiscriminately, it becomes poison.

The poisonous trap of anger is blame.

THE BLAME TRAP

"He's never on time."

My girlfriend Shana is upset.

We're in Starbucks, and she is fretting over her double decaf soy no whip latte with sugar-free almond syrup—just one pump, please.

She's that kinda girl.

"And when I've asked him, you know, why are you late, he rolls his eyes at me and tells me to take a chill pill. Chucks me on the shoulder and calls me his little control freak. Like I'm not relaxed about it enough or something." She's twisting her Starbucks napkin. "Last week, we were very late for my parents' 50th anniversary because he didn't pick me up on time." Her eyes are huge. "I mean, I have to have some say in this. It's not okay."

Hearing Shana's story, many of us will gasp in horror at Andrew's behavior. Late for your partner's parents' anniversary? How terrible! How inconsiderate! However, it might change your mind to know that Shana's version of "late" starts at exactly one minute. Andrew was ten minutes late to pick Shana up that night.

Shana and Andrew had fallen into the blame trap. In the blame trap, someone is always right, and someone is always wrong. As per Shana, if Andrew is late, then he is wrong. And for Andrew, Shana's demands seem too stringent, and therefore *she* is wrong. They each believe that both of them can't be right.

However, here is the relationship magic trick: they are *both* right.

In Shana's world, being on time makes sense and feels good. Timeliness is a form of respect. Being ten minutes late feels like two hours. However, in Andrew's world, being flexible about time makes sense. Ten minutes is nothing to get worked up about.

Both Shana and Andrew have come to logical conclusions based on their own experiences and worldviews. Their "Little Selves" have had experiences that have naturally led them to these conclusions. But from the perspective of the Big Self, neither of them is "right," and neither of them of them is "wrong." (And if you caught yourself siding with one of them, perk up and take note of your own expectations.)

We default to thinking that everyone else is like us. It's a normal bias for working in the world. We like it when others act like we do, and we figure everyone in the world is going to do things like us until we're proven otherwise. Cultivating intimacy means discovering how your person is *different* from you. Sometimes these differences seem benign: "I never knew you hated jazz, how funny!" Sometimes these differences feel like deal breakers, "I never knew you hated jazz, and I'm a jazz musician!" The road to intimacy is paved with stumbles, which is how we know that we're getting somewhere.

When someone thwarts our expectations, they are usually doing something that we wouldn't. We can be surprised, disappointed, or even angry (depending on how invested we are in what they're doing). However, it's important to understand that we're generally not upset about the actual behavior; we're upset about what we are making their behavior *mean*.

Let's use Shana and Andrew as an example. For Shana, being on time is a form of respect. Being on time *means* she's respectful. Andrew's tardiness *means* that he is being disrespectful. For Andrew, however, being flexible about time means that he is not sweating the small stuff. For him, being a bit late *means* that he's relaxed and going with the flow.

Both sets of meanings are interpretations based on Shana and Andrew's experiences. In Reality, Andrew is simply ten minutes late.

When someone's behavior irks you, take a breath and *practice the pause*. Separate their actions from what you are making the behavior mean. Rather than jumping to conclusions, investigate what the "offensive" behavior means to *the other person*. Sure, it's possible that Andrew interprets being late as a sign of disrespect, and he is unrepentantly late anyway. If that's the case, then Shana should think twice about dating him.

However, it's more probable that being late *means* something different to Andrew than to Shana.

Digging deeper into moments of conflict is an opportunity to understand someone else's point of view. Understanding where your person is coming from does not mean that you have to agree with them or tolerate their behavior, but it will give you insight into their beliefs as well as your own expectations.

Understanding the nature of anger and blame can also give you more perspective when your person is angry with *you*. When you recognize that anger is the result of thwarted expectations, then you won't take someone else's anger so personally.

Instead, you can get curious about what your person *expected* of you and why.

Mindful conflicts are the essential small tremors that relieve the pressure in a relationship; they break open the ground and create space for new discoveries.

I was so afraid of conflict during my marriage that I shut down rather than communicate. Because I shut down, I stalled out the possibility of creating an organic and ongoing dialogue about my needs. I did not understand that mindful conflict is natural, healthy, and forward moving. For a relationship to stay vital and alive, it needs to grow. Growing pains aren't comfortable, but they create the opportunity for an evolving conversation about your needs, values, and boundaries. While these conversations aren't easy, they reveal the scaffolding of our underlying assumptions, which allow us to know both our partners and ourselves better. These moments are precious opportunities to cultivate intimacy.

Literally meaning "bliss," *ananda* describes the capacity of our heart to hold even the most challenging experiences as part of our journey. *Ananda* means finding deep love regardless of the external circumstances.

BOUNDARIES

Being frightened of conflict, I was naturally afraid to establish boundaries. Tell someone what I wanted? Horror of horrors! I'd rather have pulled my teeth out.

To me, a boundary was a hard and unforgiving wall designed to separate me from another person. Boundaries were unfriendly fences that promoted selfishness, ownership, and exclusion. And wasn't love supposed to be about merging, sacrifice, and inclusion?

To understand the importance of healthy boundaries, consider the cells within your body. Cell membranes form the boundaries between the interior of your cells and the body's watery world. Having a good cellular boundary means that the cell knows what should pass through the membrane and what should be kept out. The membrane is not a rigidly erected wall; it is a discerning, organic, supple structure that invites in what is nourishing and keeps out what is harmful. What the cell needs may change over time. Without these flexible boundaries, healthy function would cease.

Viveka means "discernment" and describes our capacity to separate the beneficial from the harmful.

Similarly, in relationships, boundaries are not rigidly deflective, nor are they so porous that they lose all integrity. Boundaries invite us to be wise about what we give and what we take. What do we allow in? What do we keep out? Our health, vibrancy, and resiliency depend upon this flexible and keen discernment.

While I couldn't change my husband's drinking, I could set a boundary that would clarify what I would tolerate and what I would not. Saying, "If you drink, I will leave you," would have been a good start.

Kali

The gods and goddesses of Hinduism embody different facets of the universe and our human experience. *Kali* is a terrifying and loving goddess who reminds us that expressing great love can sometimes require courage and ferocity. She is a reminder that death is required for rebirth and transformation; we must be willing to let go in order to create something new.

Establishing boundaries with my husband would have clarified my terms of satisfaction for our marriage. He may not have done what I asked (and he may have blamed me for delivering an ultimatum), but the responsibility would then be shared. Do I want drinking more than I want Rachel? He may not have liked making a decision, but then the choice would have been his. As it was, the drinking was so muddled by the drama between us that we lacked the capacity to see where we were each accountable.

In our relationships, we get to choose: what do we let in, and what do we keep out.

When we realize that we need to create a boundary, we need a bridge across the divide. This bridge is communication.

As obvious as it might seem, your partner won't be able to honor your boundaries if they don't know what they are. Had I been able to articulate my needs in my marriage, perhaps my ex-husband and I could have hashed out some of our problems. Perhaps.

Whatever the outcome, being clear about what I could and could not tolerate would have helped *me* find a more centered sense of myself.

By communicating our boundaries, we can value our differences while upholding what we need.

Vishuddha Chakra

The throat chakra, **Vishuddha** governs our self-expression. When the energy of this chakra is over-stimulated, we ramble on and over-share our point of view. When this energy is under nourished, we are unable to find "our voice" or express our feelings. When it is well balanced, we are able to powerfully articulate who we are in the world, while at the same time leaving space for others to be heard.

In Shana's situation, she might tell Andrew, "Hon, we have a different understanding of time. However, it's important for me to get to this anniversary party before the event starts. If you don't want to pick me up on time, that's okay. But in that case, I would prefer to meet you there." Shana has taken responsibility for her own desires and her own expectations. Rather than resent Andrew for being different, she is setting up parameters that will let her be free to do what she feels that she needs to do to uphold her personal values. While Shana cannot control Andrew or change how he understands time, she can explain why promptness is important to her and make her own conditions clear. And Andrew can choose whether or not he wants to meet those conditions.

And, of course, if Shana decides that her timeliness value is a deal breaker, and Andrew doesn't want to change, then she has the choice of whether or not she wants to stay with Andrew. The most important takeaway here is to recognize that both parties are making choices.

Responsibility

As you start communicating your needs, beware of emotional manipulation or "feigning the bridge." If you are setting a boundary, then you have to set it without strings attached. If Andrew tells Shana, "Hey, pookie, you know what? I really am very lax about time, and I can't guarantee that I'll get you there when you want. It's probably better if I meet you there." Well, then it's not fair for Shana to turn around and sulk. Alternatively, if Andrew does make the choice to pick Shana up on time, then it's not fair for him to sigh grievously and feign "sacrifice."

There was a brief interval during my marriage where my husband stopped drinking. When our therapist asked him why, he pointed a finger at me: "She's making me stop." By blaming me for his decision, he got to be a victim of circumstance rather than take responsibility for his own choice.

Not taking responsibility for our own choices is a kind of lie. We are *always* responsible for our choices—even the ones that suck. Unless someone has a gun to our head, decisions cannot be forced upon us. Unfortunately, as a codependent wife, I bought into my ex-husband's victimhood spiel hook, line, and sinker. At the time, I felt guilty for "making" him do something (as if I could!). My guilt, in turn, validated his indignation, which caused me to feel guiltier, which made him feel more validated, blah blah blah. The cycle of confusion continued.

We are responsible for our choices. Even when we're dealt the worst hand in the world, we are responsible for how we play our cards. Blame and resentment are signs that we have given away the responsibility for our choice—and happiness—to someone else. They are another kind of Missing Piece confusion. In this case, rather than ascribing someone else responsibility for *our happiness*, we are blaming someone else for our *pain*.

Blame and resentment are signs that we have given responsibility for our choices—and happiness—to someone else.

"We accept the love we think we deserve."
—Stephen Chbosky, *The Perks of Being a Wallflower*

When we blame someone, we get to be the hero and make the other person the villain. My husband blamed me for his feelings and his rage. I blamed him for his drinking. We were so busy pointing fingers that we didn't address the root of the problem.

While it would be convenient to make myself the hero and my ex-husband the villain, it would not be honest. I would be doing him—and myself—a disservice. He is a good person. It's way too easy to make the world black and white; our work as yogis is to remember that the world is shades of gray. Each human in their personal virtual reality suit is doing the best they can with the experiences that they have had.

Now when I think of my ex-husband, I feel a great sense of sadness and empathy for both of us. I remember that he could be angry, resentful, and cruel. But I also remember his creativity, curiosity, and relentless passion for his art. I remember that his own experience in the darkness gave him enormous empathy for others; he devoted great energy to helping the homeless and other less fortunate people.

Remembering my ex-husband with love doesn't mean that I think we should be together. It just means that my Big Self gets to see the larger picture while I also uphold the boundaries and conditions that my Little Self needs. I can have compassion for both of us and recognize that we did the best we could. It would be easier to try to make him the bad guy, but then I would deprive myself of the opportunity to see my own responsibility as well as to see him as the whole human that he is. Choosing to see his goodness is more truthful (*satya*) and compassionate (*ahimsa*) to us both.

Having boundaries means that we can still love someone and not love their behavior. Having boundaries means that we can love someone—and ask for what we need. Having boundaries means that we can love someone—and still choose to leave them.

DATING

Dating offers us excellent practice for articulating and upholding our boundaries. From the very first text message, you are feeling out the other person's edges and establishing what kind of exchange feels good. Setting healthy boundaries from the start of a relationship creates the mutual trust and respect that will sustain your relationship as it deepens.

Signs of healthy boundaries:

- Clear, respectful communication

- He or she fits into your new life; he or she doesn't become your new life

- You make decisions because you feel good about them internally

- You are okay being alone sometimes

- You feel like you can solve your own problems

Unhealthy boundaries set up an unsteady and unsustainable foundation. While it's normal to lose yourself a little in the early stages of romance, stay alert for these signs of trouble:

- Going out of your way to be available whenever they call, no matter what's going on

- Never being available when they want your attention

- Disrespectful or dismissive communication

- Giving or taking gifts or time without integrity

- The rest of your life disappearing for one, new person

- Fuzzy expectations

- Feelings of obligation

Practice communicating your needs and expectations clearly from the start of the relationship. When you are honest about what you need, you give someone else permission to do the same. This valuable practice also allows you to take ownership of your unique expectations rather than blaming someone for not reading your mind or having different assumptions.

Practices

Journal: Anger and Fire

Journal and record when you get angry.

- Where is your anger coming from?

- What boundary is being crossed?

- What expectation is being thwarted?

Life Practice: Feel

Your anger is an opportunity to deeply feel. Rather than react to it, sit in your fire and experience the myriad of sensations in your body.

- Channel anger into action. Fuel your best vision for yourself with the potency of this energy. Rather than lash out, what's a better way to affirm what you need, or what isn't working for you?

- Sacrifice: know when to send the smoke to the gods. When it's done, it's done. Be willing to let it go.

Dating Practice: Boundaries

Practice setting boundaries that reflect your needs. From the very first text, we are communicating what is okay and not okay with us.

- Notice when you fail to uphold your own boundaries:

- Do you respond to texts at midnight?

- Are you always available?

- Do you accept all behavior without batting an eye?

If your boundaries fail, do you know why? Was it for a good reason? How could you support yourself to uphold them?

Meditation Practice: Boundaries

We often have a hard time setting boundaries because we are afraid. For your meditation practice, choose one word (*mantra*) that evokes a sense of your inner power. For example, you could choose a word such as "strength," "power," "goddess," or "clarity."

- Find your meditation seat (see chapter two for more detailed instructions if needed).

- Follow your breath.

- On each inhale and exhale, repeat your chosen mantra silently to yourself.

- After about five minutes, take a few normal breaths and notice how you feel.

Yoga Practice: Boundaries

- Locust

- Floor bow

Feel the fire of your practice. Use the connection of your hands to create more space and opening through your heart. Notice how the strength of your boundaries (the hands together, the connection of your legs, the rooting of the pelvis into the floor) facilitates greater space and ease.

Chapter 13
LOVE

Relationships require commitment.

And commitment can be scary.

After my relationship with Mikey the DJ, I was very wary of commitment. In retrospect, the logic is obvious:

- Because I was scared of conflict, I had crap boundaries.

- Having crap boundaries mean that I swallowed my feelings and stayed silent, which led to me getting hurt.

- After that experience, it was easier to avoid relationships entirely than to deal with a situation where I might self-sabotage.

Of course, I didn't understand this pattern *consciously*. I dated, but I stayed away from anyone who looked like a serious contender. I dismissed nice guys as "boring" and chose scoundrels that I couldn't take seriously. I dated nineteen-year-olds like Mercutio who were easy to control. No one who could be truly threatening, thank you very much.

Then I fell in love with Franklin.

Quite by accident.

Love snuck up on me during a four-month acting tour. Had I not been around him every day, it never would have happened. But when you're traveling around the United States in a van with eight other actors, hauling your own sets, doing your own makeup, wearing ridiculous wigs, and defiling a perfectly innocent Molière play by speaking bad French to middle school students ... well, that kind of experience bonds you.

Franklin looked like a gawky version of Edward Norton, quiet and unassuming. I watched him from a safe distance as he performed a million small kindnesses for everyone each day. He was a true gentleman: humble and unfailingly good. I fell for him completely.

After the tour, Franklin and I lived together in New York City before I received the big news: I'd been accepted to earn my master of fine arts in acting at the American Conservatory Theater.

Getting accepted to the program was a big deal. There were only eighteen spots in my class. Franklin and I tried to hold the relationship together across three thousand miles and three years, but, of course, there were challenges. With no language to discuss my ambivalence, I withdrew into silence. Once again, I did not know how to navigate uncertainty, even though I loved him. I thought that my complicated feelings meant that the relationship wasn't working. After agonizing (privately, of course) for several months, I suddenly broke our relationship off.

Years later, still in love with him (and beginning to have a dim idea that relationships might be more complicated than "all" or "nothing"), I called him to ask if there was any chance for us. Had he moved on? By that time, of course he had.

It's taken me a long time to begin to understand the nature of commitment.

I had always thought of a commitment as a rock whose power came from its rigidity and imperviousness to change. Commitments were airtight, vacuum-sealed, and perfectly preserved. Cracks in the armor were not permitted. My stiff ideas about commitment were undoubtedly informed by my ex-Marine dad (Semper Fi), who "did the right thing" without complaint until he drowned his feelings in vodka.

To be willing to say yes to a relationship, I had to redefine my understanding of commitment.

I remember the moment that I decided to open myself up to falling in love with Alex. Even after we had started sleeping together, I had been keeping my emotional distance. I was afraid of getting hurt.

Then I took a trip home to the family farm for Christmas.

I sat in the heart of my family's love, participated in our silly squabbles, and enjoyed being with my wonderful dad (who, with the help of AA, had pulled himself out of the devil's teeth). Here was my family, so loving and supportive, but also ridiculous and human and messy. We had come through so much together. And through our challenges, we had grown closer.

I'd been waiting for love to arrive in a neat, symmetrical box. But love may arrive gift wrapped in wild and unruly packaging.

When I returned to Vancouver, I took a breath and decided to open my heart to Alex.

"Uhhhhh, what's going on?" Alex asks me.

"What do you mean?"

He sounds perplexed. "Ever since you got back you've been calling me. Making plans, showing up ..."

"Yeah. Well, isn't that good?"

"Well, yeah, it's good ... but ..."

"But what?"

"It's different. From how it was. You're kinda freaking me out."

"I'm freaking you out?"

"Yeah, well, what's changed? Should we talk about this?"

I think for a moment. "I decided to say yes," I finally say. "I decided to say yes to this, to us. I decided to stop running from my fear and instead see what happens."

He looks at me. "Oh. Okay then."

"This is me showing up."

"That's great. But ... I'm still a little freaked out."

"Yeah, totally," I say, "I'm freaked out too."

Saying yes to *romance* is easy; saying yes to *love* takes courage. When we say yes to love, we are saying "yes" knowing that our relationship with another person is not going to fix our problems or follow a neat plan. Our practice navigating the uncertainty of dating has laid the strong foundation that we need to now embark upon a journey of the heart.

I now understand that a *wholesome* commitment must let the air and light in. There must be flow, new information, and recalibrations. Wholesome commitments are not black and white; they are organic, messy, and flexible. There will be conflict, doubt, and ambiguity. The process of navigating this messiness is precisely what helps us cultivate intimacy and become closer to our partners. Relationships, like everything in nature (*prakriti*), move and change. To be alive, they must be allowed to evolve.

Wholesome commitments are made of bamboo, not iron. To remain vital, a commitment stays true to its intent but has the space to be re-imagined and newly understood. A commitment is an active and ongoing choice, not a passive obligation. It is powerful and enduring when it is deliberately affirmed.

In a wholesome commitment, we stay to uphold our values, we stay to uphold ourselves, and we may stay to uphold someone else.

We don't stay just because we said so.

Your Beautiful Heart

Love is governed by *anahata chakra,* the heart's energetic center.

As we move from the earthly chakra in the pelvis to the etheric chakra at the crown of the head, the energies of the chakras become progressively more refined. The heart chakra is poised in the center of the body. It is the middle chakra, balanced between pelvis and crown, earth and sky. The heart negotiates the relationship between the physical world and our spiritual understanding.

Anahata chakra is our heart center and is located in the very center of the chakra system. It is the midway point between the lower three chakras (relating to the energy of the material world) and the etheric elements (relating to the energy of the spiritual world). *Anahata* is the bridge between the earth and sky.

Anahata means "unstruck" and reminds us that the nature of the heart—and our Big Self—is pure, unharmed, and free. *Anahata* is about negotiating balance; our heart chakra governs how we both receive and express love. If we are over expressive in this center, we may lose ourselves in someone else. If we are deficient in this center, we may withhold and contract.

Anahata governs our ability to engage in healthy exchange, compassion, to give as well as receive from others. Governed by air and movement, the power of *anahata* radiates from our heart. Expressed through our arms and hands, *anahata's* energy is made physical through how we touch the world.

The heart is the bridge between our earthly humanity and our connection to the divine. The heart is a pivot point, an opportunity to embody our spiritual values and put them into practice in the world. The heart chakra is governed by the element of air, which is constantly moving. Like the lungs that snuggle the heart, the expression of love is not fixed. There is a constant inhale and exhale, expansion and contraction, reception and offering.

Spanda means "divine vibration," and describes the inherent pulsation of the universe. *Spanda* reminds us that the universe is always in a state of change, of contraction, and of expansion. We will connect and disconnect. We will feel passion, then we will feel distance, then passion once again. All these fluctuations are part of the universal heartbeat.

Love is not static; it flows.

Love is not an idea; it is an action.

LEARNING TO STAY

A wise woman once said to me, "Most relationships end when the other person stops covering up our inner feeling of unworthiness."

Yikes.

But true.

Most relationships fall into a Missing Piece confusion at some point. We start depending on our partner to be a certain way for us to feel safe. When the other person stops acting the way we want, then we might get upset and say that the relationship is not working. The deal is broken, we fall out of love. The relationship has "serious problems" and "irreconcilable differences."

Don't freak out. This is normal.

Our work as yogis is to stay awake, *practice the pause*, and try to figure out what's really happening. Is there really a deal breaker here? Or have we turned our partner into an emotional security blanket?

Our work is to persistently, gently, and humbly return to the present moment. Take a breath and put our Big Self back in the driver's seat. From that vantage point, we can see the other person for who they are rather than just for who we want them to be. This is the starting point of unconditional love.

My yoga teacher has a good story to describe the power of a consistent yoga practice, and it applies equally well to relationships.

Let's imagine that you want to dig a well in order to get water. You start digging in one place that seems good. At first, it's exciting! Yay! A well! But then it gets boring. You get tired. It starts becoming *work*. So you think, eh, this hole sucks. I'm going somewhere else that's better. And you start digging a new hole in a different place. Ah, good. At first this place seems much better. Then you run into a rock, and the digging gets hard again. So you pull up your stakes and start digging somewhere else. And so on, and so on. Soon you've got a field full of holes and no water.

Abhyasa means, "practice." In the **Yoga Sutra**, "practice" has the following conditions: consistency, devotion, and endurance. Like a relationship, practice doesn't happen when it's convenient or just feels good. Our relationships are invitations to practice mindful steadiness. By committing, we discover in ourselves a deep well of love and strength that allows us to be present through all the colors of our experience.

Being in a committed relationship is like digging a well. If we give up when we hit the first tough spot, we're never going to find the water. When we move from one relationship to another rather than digging past the rocks, we deprive ourselves of the opportunity to see what's on the other side, to find the water, to earn the fruits of our labor. Freedom can only be found through commitment.

To be clear, I am not suggesting that you bear out terrible circumstances in order to "learn a lesson." There are times that you're going to have to leave your half-dug well—and good riddance! But it's better to leave with clarity than reactivity.

Yoga

From the root word "yuj"—to bind or yoke. Through binding, we find freedom.

Dharana

The first stage of meditation, *dharana* (concentration) requires steadfastness. Just as in relationships, we return patiently, persistently, and curiously to the experience of the present moment, even when we are uncomfortable and want to be distracted. By remaining awake and present, we nourish the field of our relationship and cultivate a deep sense of trust and resiliency with our partner.

When we commit ourselves to anything—whether it's a relationship, guitar playing, our kids, our yoga, or our work— we start to find the edges of our capacity. We find our grit. We find out where we want to bail and figure out how we can stick it out. We fail. And we try again. And through our efforts, we start to uncover our inner strength. When we flit from thing to thing, we never find out who we really are. We never get to the juice.

Trust is built when we stay despite the changes, the ups and downs. When we can hit a rock and not rebound into reaction. Not only do we begin to trust our partners, but we start to trust ourselves. Beneath the shifting sands of our feelings and cravings, we discover our consistency and stability.

We have found the water.

HOPE

Learning to stay means *letting go of hope.*

I know this invitation sounds pretty unappealing. However, if you remember from chapter two, intimacy is the opposite of romance. Romance thrives on the unknown (oh, the heights we can imagine!), while intimacy grows in an authentic, compassionate understanding of another person.

Letting go of hope is an invitation to give up fantasy in favor of the possibility and power of the present moment. Learning to stay means letting go of the romantic notion that there is something better that we're missing out on, a greener lawn just around the corner.

This moment is the opportunity. Change, compassion, action cannot happen in the future or in the past or in an imagined alter life. *Now* is the portal to all action. This life—your life—has put you exactly where you are supposed to be. When you bind yourself to this moment, you are embracing Reality. You are choosing—now, and now, and now—be your best self, your bravest self. One moment at a time.

Samadhi is the culmination of meditation and describes the absorption that is the result of steadiness over time. *Samadhi* is integration, a blissful state that is the result of steadfastness.

From Wholeness, Relationship

When I began my dating adventures, I was looking for "the one."

I wanted—needed—to fix my problems by finding someone else to fill the missing gaps, to make me feel safe, and to hold me tight against the storm. I wanted children in order to feel that I was living a complete life. And I needed the partner to fit my idea of "perfect" in order to make my dream of a life finally come true. My expectations had to be fulfilled in order to feel that I was successful. I needed a house, two kids, a loving husband, and a banging career. Then I'd finally be able to wipe my brow. Phew!

Crashing on the shores of my own expectations and entitlement was an awakening. Terrible, beautiful, and cleansing, like a winter storm off a rocky, windswept coast. By trying again and again to find happiness in others, I finally saw myself.

The riddle of my happiness will never be solved by someone else. For better and for worse, in sickness and in health, I am my own complex and lovely puzzle to figure out.

Needing someone else in order to be whole is not love.

Ultimately, no one—and nothing—can completely fulfill our deep longing. The human condition is to be sweetly imperfect, continually on a knife's edge, desperate to hold on to something in the outside world to make us feel okay. Until we soften to this uncertainty and open our hearts to our continual restlessness, we will repeat our grasping patterns. Rather than waiting for a hero, we can gently accept that we are the ones who ultimately must show up for ourselves and hold ourselves in the dark. Although this doesn't mean that someone else can't also hold your hand.

By increasing your capacity to hold space for yourself, you release others from the obligation to fix you. When you stand in yourself, then you can see someone else for who they are— rather than who you want or need them to be. *This* is unconditional love. This is intimacy.

Unconditional love supports someone else to engage in his or her own soul's journey. You can see your partner as a magnificent human being, full of hopes, dreams, stumbles, and aspirations. You can help them breathe through their unfinished business, lean into the darkness, and emerge more fully into the light.

When we arrive in our relationships knowing (or at least trying to remember!) that we are already whole, then we can nourish and support someone else from a place of generosity rather than negotiation.

We will naturally falter.

We will naturally forget.

But yoga helps us to remember our deep and centered intrinsic wholeness. When we love our person from this deep well, we can be truly supportive: ready to engage in mutual discovery and growth.

SPIRITUAL LOVE

Love is a spiritual opportunity.

Once you have opened the door of self-inquiry, you are committed. Your soul is hungry and curious to dive deeper, understand more, and lean in. You cannot close your eyes to the depths that you have already excavated.

The human heart wants to choose love over fear. Love invites us to find the best of our humanity, to witness another's process with kindness and curiosity, to support them in their path rather than our own agenda. Our capacity to love is a precious gift. When we connect with others, our most refined qualities—compassion, empathy, sacrifice, generosity—are expressed.

God realization is not something that happens only in prayer or deep meditation. Realizing God in this world emerges from our participation every day in our relationships, in how we touch and reach each other. Each one of us is a reflection of Universal Consciousness, and our opportunity is to create the change that we want to see in the world, one moment at a time. Though this is a practice that is starkly visible in our intimate relationships, we can engage in this practice in every moment.

Sahasrara

The crown chakra, **sahasrara** is the energetic center that governs our relationship with God. This center enables us to connect beyond the bounds of our individual identity and begin to experience our connection to the great web of Universal Consciousness. We are part of a great unfolding. We are part of something bigger. And we are an expression of the divine.

We are weavers. Our interactions, words, and gestures are the threads that we use to create the grand tapestry of our lives. We are weaving the world into creation with every act and word. Cultivating integrity in our relationships is not just about expressing love to a partner; we are *elevating all of humanity*. The extra breath that we take before reacting creates more peace. Catching our imaginations at work creates more accountability. Listening with care creates more empathy. Acting from the Big Self creates more love.

We do not weave alone.

While our work is to remember our own self-sufficiency, our joy is to reach out, connect, love, and elevate each other in this creative work. Our own weaving is but a small part of the grand universal tapestry that is being created in concert with the rest of humanity in every single moment. How we support each other on the journey matters. We are in this glorious act of creation together.

In yoga, we often speak of *kula*, or community.

Kula

"A community, clan, or family." In yoga, we often think of a **kula** as our spiritual community, which comes together with a shared intention and purpose. A **kula** is a gathering of like-minded people who support each other on the path. Within a **kula**, we find a trustworthy support network to wrestle with spiritual questions and support each other through the challenges of daily life.

Your *kula* is the community of your heart; it includes your cherished friends, family, loved ones, and fellow yogis. Through community, we have the opportunity to support each other in upholding our most precious values.

Maya is the veil of illusion that causes us to see ourselves as separate from everything, rather than recognizing that we are all part of a divine whole. Beyond the illusion, everything is one.

Love is not about one person; love is expressed in all of our relationships. With family, with friends, with strangers. From our understanding of our own intrinsic wholeness, we have a greater capacity to lean into relationships. Not just our relationship with a lover, but also our relationship with the world. Not just being our best for one person, but also being our best for everyone. Not just leaning into the tenderness and softness of one heart, but all hearts.

Your practice in dating is merely foreplay, if you will.

Now take everything you know into your waking life. Into every relationship. Into each of your daily moments.

Catch yourself in your daydreams, speak your truth when honesty feels scary, uphold your boundaries, recognize your past, enjoy your sensual pleasures, and trust in the great unfolding of your life. Not only are you a child of the universe, but you are also *creating* the universe in every moment, with every action, with every breath. You are that.

You. Are. That.

Our humanity is to forget.

Our practice is to remember.

"Tell me, what is it you plan to do with your one wild and precious life?"
—Mary Oliver

Practices

Journal: Commitment

- Where in your life have you followed through on an important commitment? How did that feel?

- A good relationship should give us more freedom to be who we want to be—not less. Write out your fears:

    o What scares you the most about being committed to someone?

    o What are you afraid that you will lose?

    o Now examine your greatest fear. What if it's not true?

Journal: Mission

- Come back to the mission statement that you wrote in chapter four. Brainstorm again and redraft.

- Revisit your values. What are they?

- What would your values look like in action? With a loved one? At work? With a stranger?

Meditation Practice: Persistence

For the next week, commit to doing a 2–5 minute meditation every day. You can use any meditation that speaks to you. The meditation does not need to be perfect. As you commit to a daily practice, notice what obstacles you face. If you fail, then simply start again the next day without judgment or recrimination. Now is the time. It's not about being perfect but about renewing our dedication to showing up.

Meditation Practice: Heart Opening

- Come into comfortable meditation seat (see chapter two for more detailed instructions if needed).

- Settle in for a few minutes, focusing on your breath.

- Bring to mind the face of someone whom you love very much. Visualize this person. Repeat to yourself, "Just like me, you want to be happy."

- Bring to mind the face of someone about whom you feel neutral. Visualize this person. Repeat to yourself, "Just like me, you want to be happy."

- Bring to mind the face of someone with whom you experience emotional challenges. Visualize this person. Repeat to yourself, "Just like me, you want to be happy."

- Slowly begin to expand your consciousness to a wider net of people (your house, your town, your state, your country, the world). With each expansion, hold them in your heart and repeat to yourself, "Just like me, you want to be happy."

- Let the visualization go and take a few deeps breaths.

- How do you feel?

Yoga Practice: Sweet Unfolding

- Pigeon

- Seated twist

- Forward fold

- Savasana

- Meditation

It's time to let go and relax into the sweet unfolding. The work is done. Now is the time to rest in the fruits of your efforts. As you practice these poses, come to your sensible edge and then practice softening there. Do not rush. Give yourself time to stay. Use each exhale to sense how mindful surrender can deepen your experience.

$\mathcal{THE}$
EPILOGUE

At the time of writing of this book, I am participating in a donor insemination program. Donor insemination is where you buy and insert (uh, insert? Would that be the word?) sperm from a sperm bank into your uterus to try to get pregnant. This is one step short of in-vitro fertilization, where they remove eggs from your body, externally fertilize the egg, and then put it back in. You can choose your donor from a catalogue, see his picture, hear his voice. It's pretty wild.

If I can have a child at the age of forty-three or forty-four, then I will be a mom. If I cannot, then I will take the energy that I would give that child and lavish it as best I can on the beautiful people that I love. I am doing my best to walk down the path and let my heart – and the Universe-decide.

As for relationships?

When Alex and I broke up, I completely fell apart. With him, my dreams for a family and kids had come alive again—so vividly! I could touch them. When we broke up, it felt like my final hopes for a traditional marriage were finally shattered. I had panic attacks and depressive episodes. I cut myself. Just once, but it happened. I felt suicidal. Everything in my life felt dull, gray, and dead.

During this difficult time, I started compiling my stories and writing this book (*Head Over Heels: A Yogi's Guide to Dating*). As I wrote and edited the chapters, I was reminded that—even though I felt as if I had lost my way—there was a part of me that did know the path. I'd read a chapter and think, "Damn, that's a good idea! Well, I better put on my big girl pants and follow my own advice."

Part of our work is to practice self-love and be willing to humbly learn the same lessons again, and again, and again.

I came to realize that I had been dependent on Alex to "fix" me, as if I were broken. I had been relying on the fulfillment of my family dream to complete me. Yes, I felt loss for this man, but I had also fallen into the Missing Piece trap. Again.

I realized that any relationship that I started at this point in my life would be under terrible pressure: "Will you have children with me now? Can you fix my problem?" After my relationship with Alex, I couldn't fathom being able to create the trust and love necessary to build a relationship within my remaining window of (possible) fertility.

Perhaps the baby needed to come first?

For many months, I agonized about whether or not I should pursue having a child on my own. Was I seeking a child out of fear, or out of love? Was I afraid of being alone? Was I being selfish? What was the best choice? After months of contemplation and conversation, I realized that I was looking at two visions for my future.

- In vision one, I was old, afraid, and incompetent. I had no support or allies. I had limited resources. The future felt small and contracted.

- In vision two, I was healthy, vibrant, and resourceful. I had a community of loving family and friends. I felt expansive and full of love.

I chose vision two.

So we will see.

And regardless of whether or not I have my own child, I will practice living vision two.

THE GENTLEMEN

In case you were wondering.

Alex: Alex and I are still in touch, and I still wonder if there's more that we could have done to figure the relationship out. He continues to go on wonderful adventures and is doing well.

Zach: "Goodly brick of cheese." He was my first friend to help me through the horrors of my divorce. I'll tell you now that he is my ex-boyfriend (we broke up when I was thirty-nine). He sees my frailties and strengths and loves people madly from his giant heart. He does not want children.

Champagne Steve: Contacted me a year later to ask me out again. I went out with him, and he was (sort of) apologetic about what had happened. He wanted to date again. I declined after I realized that I don't trust him.

My Ex-Husband: I haven't spoken to him since our divorce. Sometimes fire destroys the bridges.

Curt: "Had a great time till you kicked me in the balls." Curt contacted me about a year later to check in. He is very kind and a good guy. Also—very gentlemanly—he let me know that someone was posting false profiles of me on OkCupid.

Lucas: Date who reminded me of my cousin. He got back together with his ex-girlfriend.

Jeremy: The filmmaker. After seven years, I finally told him that I didn't feel like he was there for me as a friend. He apologized, said he wanted to try, and then disappeared. His career is going extremely well.

Ethan: First Tinder date. I haven't spoken to him since he told me that he was seeing someone else.

Michael: The polyamorist. Turned out he also dated a friend of mine briefly. My girlfriend and I had a good giggle.

Brant: "Great first date but no spark." Kept texting me. I eventually blocked him.

Mikey the DJ: High school boyfriend. We connected after college and had a heart to heart about our teenage challenges. He's still a DJ, is married, and doing well.

Geoff: First kiss. Has a beautiful family and is doing well.

Franklin: First love. Has a beautiful family and is doing well.

Suggestions
FOR READING

The Artist's Way, Julia Cameron

The Places That Scare You, Pema Chodron

When Things Fall Apart, Pema Chodron

The Great Work of Your Life, Stephen Cope

The Buddha's Brain, Rick Hansen

Coming to Our Senses, Jon Kabat-Zinn

Touching Enlightenment, Reginald Ray

The Yoga Sutras of Patanjali, Sri Swami Satchidananda

Wit and Wisdom From The Yoga Mat, Rachel Scott (my first book!)

Fierce Kindness: Be A Positive Force For Change, Melanie Salvatore-August

More Library Suggestions can be found at Rachelyoga.com

About the
AUTHOR

Ah, if you've read the book you know everything!

Rachel is an author, yoga teacher, speaker, and educational nerd based in Vancouver, BC. When she's not cheerleading her students to better relationships, she loves helping yoga teachers find their voice and develop their skills. As an educational designer, she supports passionate yogis and studio owners create dynamic and effective educational experiences. She has personally taught over twenty 200-hour yoga teacher trainings and created hundreds of hours of curriculum.

A dual citizen of Canada and the United States, you can often find her in Texas at her parents' farm where she tries to pet the chickens. She sings opera for fun.

E-RYT 500; BA Columbia University; Masters of Fine Arts, Acting; Masters of Science, Instructional Systems and Learning Technologies.

Let's Work
TOGETHER

Want more? Here are some ways we can work together.

- Yoga students and teachers: check out the free classes and extensive online resources at RachelYoga.com.

- Looking for a fun, real and expressive motivational speaker? Contact Rachel at info@rachelyoga.com.

- Teachers and studios: want to share your passion? Transform your knowledge and skills into a smart, savvy, and dynamic teacher training. Whether you are creating or refining, I will help you create the program of your dreams.

Find out more at:
theartofyogaeducation.com.

Rachel Scott • 247

Love this book?

If you loved this book, please jump onto Amazon by going to:

http://a.co/cvL6kba

and share your review! Your kind words are my best testimonials and help spread the love.

Made in the USA
Middletown, DE
18 December 2019